United States Government Accountability Office

Report to Congressional Committees

I0426220

July 2012

U.S. MERCHANT MARINE ACADEMY

Additional Actions Needed to Establish Effective Internal Control

GAO

Accountability ★ Integrity ★ Reliability

GAO-12-369

Highlights of GAO-12-369, a report to congressional committees

U.S. MERCHANT MARINE ACADEMY

Additional Actions Needed to Establish Effective Internal Control

Why GAO Did This Study

The Academy, a component of the Department of Transportation's (DOT) MARAD, was established in 1938 and built during World War II to provide undergraduate education programs for midshipmen to become shipboard officers and leaders in the maritime transportation field. DOT allocated $80 million to the Academy for fiscal year 2011 for its operations, CIP, and facilities maintenance.

In August 2009, GAO issued a report that identified numerous internal control deficiencies and made 47 recommendations for corrective action. This report provides the results of GAO's assessment of (1) the extent to which the Academy has taken actions to address the prior recommendations and (2) the Academy's CIP oversight. To address these objectives, GAO evaluated corrective actions and supporting documentation; interviewed Academy, MARAD, and DOT officials; and performed walk-throughs of several processes revised in response to GAO's prior recommendations.

What GAO Recommends

In addition to reiterating the need to fully implement the remaining open recommendations, GAO is making one new recommendation directed at updating the Academy's capital improvement plan to include reliable cost estimates and phased investment priorities aligned with the Academy's strategic objectives in accordance with leading practices. In commenting on a draft of this report, DOT stated that it had recently established a comprehensive plan to manage CIP, and plans to keep GAO apprised as it completes actions addressing other GAO open recommendations.

View GAO-12-369. For more information, contact Beryl Davis at (202) 512-2600 or DavisBH@gao.gov.

What GAO Found

The U.S. Merchant Marine Academy (Academy) has made progress in improving its internal control since GAO's August 2009 report, but has not yet fully addressed one key recommendation related to fundamental weaknesses in its overall internal control system. GAO found that while the Academy had appointed an Internal Control Officer responsible for coordinating reviews of internal controls, it had not yet established a comprehensive risk-based internal control system to ensure effective and efficient operations, reliable financial reporting, and compliance with laws and regulations, including a monitoring system to help ensure that control deficiencies are proactively identified and promptly corrected. Maritime Administration (MARAD) officials stated that their strategy had been to focus on the deficiencies that could be readily resolved. As of September 30, 2011, Academy and MARAD officials had addressed 32 of the other 46 prior recommendations regarding control activity deficiencies.

Summary of GAO Conclusion on Status of Actions Taken to Address 2009 Recommendations Related to the Academy's Control Activities

Academy control activity	Total recommendations	Recommendations implemented	Remaining open recommendations
Training vessel use	5	5	0
Personal service acquisitions	2	2	0
NAFI camps and clinics using Academy facilities	3	3	0
Midshipmen fee accountability	9	7	2
Accountability for Academy reserves	4	4	0
Academy and NAFI governance structure	8	4	4
Financial reporting	5	2	3
Fund accountability	7	4	3
Capital asset repairs and improvements	3	1	2
Total	**46**	**32**	**14**

Source: GAO analysis of MARAD and Academy data as of September 30, 2011.

Importantly, for many of the specific control-related recommendations that remained open, the Academy and MARAD had not yet identified the cause of the related internal control deficiencies, a critical step for designing effective controls.

GAO also found that the Academy and MARAD have taken steps to improve Capital Improvement Program (CIP) oversight. For example, the Academy filled a new Assistant Superintendent position responsible for oversight of the Academy's capital improvements and facilities maintenance. However, the Academy did not yet have an up-to-date, comprehensive plan for capital improvements to provide a basis for oversight. Specifically, the Academy did not have a capital improvement plan that identified long-term capital improvement needs aligned with the Academy's strategic objectives, reliable cost estimates for planned improvements, and a phased implementation approach for prioritizing capital improvement needs. Such plan elements are consistent with Office of Management and Budget guidance and GAO-identified leading practices.

_____ United States Government Accountability Office

Contents

Abbreviations

ADA	Antideficiency Act
CFO	Chief Financial Officer
CIP	Capital Improvement Program
DOT	Department of Transportation
FAR	Federal Acquisition Regulation
FCO	Fiscal Control Office
FMFIA	Federal Managers' Financial Integrity Act
FOB	Fiscal Oversight Board
GMATS	Global Maritime and Transportation School
ICO	Internal Control Officer
MAO	Maritime Administrative Order
MARAD	Maritime Administration
NAFI	Nonappropriated Fund Instrumentality
R&M	Repair and Maintenance

United States Government Accountability Office
Washington, DC 20548

July 6, 2012

The Honorable Patty Murray
Chairman
The Honorable Susan M. Collins
Ranking Member
Subcommittee on Transportation, Housing and Urban Development,
    and Related Agencies
Committee on Appropriations
United States Senate

The Honorable Tom Latham
Chairman
The Honorable John W. Olver
Ranking Member
Subcommittee on Transportation, Housing and Urban Development,
    and Related Agencies
Committee on Appropriations
House of Representatives

The U.S. Merchant Marine Academy (Academy), one of five United States service academies, was established in 1938 to provide 4-year undergraduate educational programs for men and women (midshipmen) to become shipboard officers and leaders in the maritime transportation field. A graduate from the Academy receives a Bachelor of Science degree and a U.S. Coast Guard license as deck or engineering officer and a commission in the U.S. Naval Reserve or another uniformed service. The Academy is a component of, and receives federal funding and overall policy direction through, the Department of Transportation's (DOT) Maritime Administration (MARAD). For fiscal year 2011, DOT allocated $80 million to the Academy for its operations, capital improvements, and facilities maintenance. Most of the Academy's 44 principal facilities were constructed during or shortly after World War II.

In August 2009, we issued a report[1] that identified numerous deficiencies in the Academy's internal control activities and weaknesses in the

---

[1]GAO, *United States Merchant Marine Academy: Internal Control Weaknesses Resulted in Improper Sources and Uses of Funds; Some Corrective Actions Are Under Way*, GAO-09-635 (Washington, D.C.: Aug. 10, 2009).

Academy's overall internal control environment[2] that resulted in numerous instances of improper and questionable sources and uses of funds by the Academy and its affiliated organizations. Our 2009 report included 47 recommendations to address the deficiencies we identified. You requested that we update the status of the Academy's efforts to address our recommendations from our 2009 report and that we review the Academy's oversight of its Capital Improvement Program (CIP).[3] This report provides the results of our assessment of (1) the extent to which the Academy has taken actions to address our prior recommendations and (2) the Academy's CIP oversight.

To assess the extent to which actions have been taken to address our prior recommendations, we (1) evaluated the Academy's and MARAD's corrective actions for each recommendation and supporting documentation as of September 30, 2011, and—where relevant—reviewed documentation supporting selected transactions to assess the Academy's implementation of revised internal control procedures; (2) interviewed Academy, MARAD, and DOT officials responsible for the development and implementation of the corrective actions; and (3) performed walk-throughs of the Academy's processes as revised in response to our recommendations.

To assess the Academy's oversight of its CIP, we (1) interviewed cognizant agency officials responsible for oversight of the Academy's implementation of the program, (2) obtained and reviewed related policies and procedures and strategic planning documents, and (3) toured the Academy grounds to observe the current physical condition of buildings and infrastructure. In addition, we interviewed MARAD human resources

---

[2]GAO, *Standards for Internal Control in the Federal Government*, GAO/AIMD-00-21.3.1 (Washington, D.C.: November 1999). *Standards for Internal Control in the Federal Government* provides that the control environment sets the tone of the organization, influencing the control consciousness of its people and their attitude toward internal control. It is the foundation for all other components of internal control, providing discipline and structure. Control environment factors include the integrity, ethical values, and competence of the entity's people; management's philosophy and operating style; and the way management assigns authority and responsibility and organizes and develops its people.

[3]The Academy's CIP encompasses the construction or maintenance of capital assets at the Academy, including construction of new academic or support facilities, major renovation or refurbishment of existing facilities, or acquisition or replacement of capital equipment or training resource needs.

personnel regarding Academy staff resources used to oversee and manage CIP projects.

During our review, the Academy and MARAD continued to address internal control weaknesses that were the focus of our prior recommendations. For this report, we evaluated corrective actions taken through September 30, 2011, that the Academy, MARAD, and DOT made us aware of as of February 15, 2012. We will evaluate information that we receive about additional actions taken as part of our standard, ongoing recommendation follow-up procedures.

We conducted this performance audit from February 2011 to June 2012 in accordance with generally accepted government auditing standards. Those standards require that we plan and perform the audit to obtain sufficient, appropriate evidence to provide a reasonable basis for our findings and conclusions based on our audit objectives. We believe that the evidence obtained provides a reasonable basis for our findings and conclusions based on our audit objectives. Additional details on our scope and methodology are in appendix I.

Background

Organizational Structure and Oversight

MARAD is responsible for overall policy direction of the Academy. The Maritime Administrator issues Maritime Administrative Orders (MAO) and bulletins establishing policies and providing guidelines for Academy operations. Additionally, the MARAD Chief Financial Officer (CFO) issues directives to provide guidance for conducting Academy financial operations. Since 2010, there have been two MARAD CFOs with an acting CFO between their appointments. From 2009 through 2011, MARAD relied on a Fiscal Oversight Board to assist MARAD in the oversight of the Academy's operations.

The Academy Superintendent is responsible for day-to-day management of the Academy and reports directly to the head of MARAD, the Maritime Administrator. Since September 2008, there have been three Academy Superintendents, with the Academic Dean serving as Interim

Superintendent between Superintendent appointments.[4] Various assistant superintendents report to the Superintendent, and various directors of departments and offices report to the assistant superintendents. The Office of Academy Operations is led by the Academy's CFO, who reports directly to the MARAD CFO. Additionally, since our 2009 report, four Academy support functions[5] now report directly to MARAD headquarters offices.

As of September 30, 2011, the Academy was also affiliated with two nonappropriated fund instrumentalities (NAFI) intended to assist the Academy in providing programs and services primarily for Academy midshipmen and employees. One of these NAFIs, the Employee Association, is intended to promote and support the interests of Academy personnel. The other is the Regimental Morale Fund Association, authorized to support morale, welfare, and recreation activities for the Academy's midshipmen. In addition, as of September 30, 2011, four other NAFIs were in transition for closure (see table 1).

Table 1: NAFIs in Transition for Closure

NAFI	Purpose	Status
Global Maritime and Transportation School	Provide education and training to other federal agencies and to the maritime industry.	MARAD rescinded this NAFI's authorization but authorized transitional operations through its planned closure on July 31, 2012.
Melville Hall	Provide dining, lodging, and meeting facilities.	MARAD rescinded this NAFI's authorization but authorized transitional operations through its planned closure on October 31, 2012, to complete conversion to a contract agreement.
Athletics Association	Enhance midshipmen's educational experience through participation in athletic activities.	MARAD rescinded this NAFI's authorization but authorized transitional operations through its planned closure on December 31, 2011, to complete transition to an appropriated federal program.
Fiscal Control Office (FCO)	Provide bookkeeping, payroll, and other administrative support services for NAFIs.	MARAD rescinded this NAFI's authorization on March 16, 2010. The Academy CFO assumed the FCO NAFI's responsibilities for the administrative and financial functions of the NAFIs in transition for closure until they cease operations completely.

Source: GAO presentation of MARAD data as of September 30, 2011.

---

[4]In addition, on June 25, 2012, the Secretary of Transportation announced that a new Superintendent had been appointed and would begin work at the Academy in July 2012.
[5]The four Academy support offices that report directly to MARAD are the Offices of Academy Operations, Procurement, Human Resources, and Academy Legal Counsel.

Additionally, the Academy also received financial support from two private foundations, the U.S. Merchant Marine Academy Alumni Association and Foundation and the Sailing Foundation. These foundations use funds provided by Academy alumni to provide financial support for the Academy's charitable, scientific, and educational activities. See figure 1 for an overview of DOT, MARAD, and Academy organizational relationships.

Figure 1: Overview of Merchant Marine Academy Organizational Structure

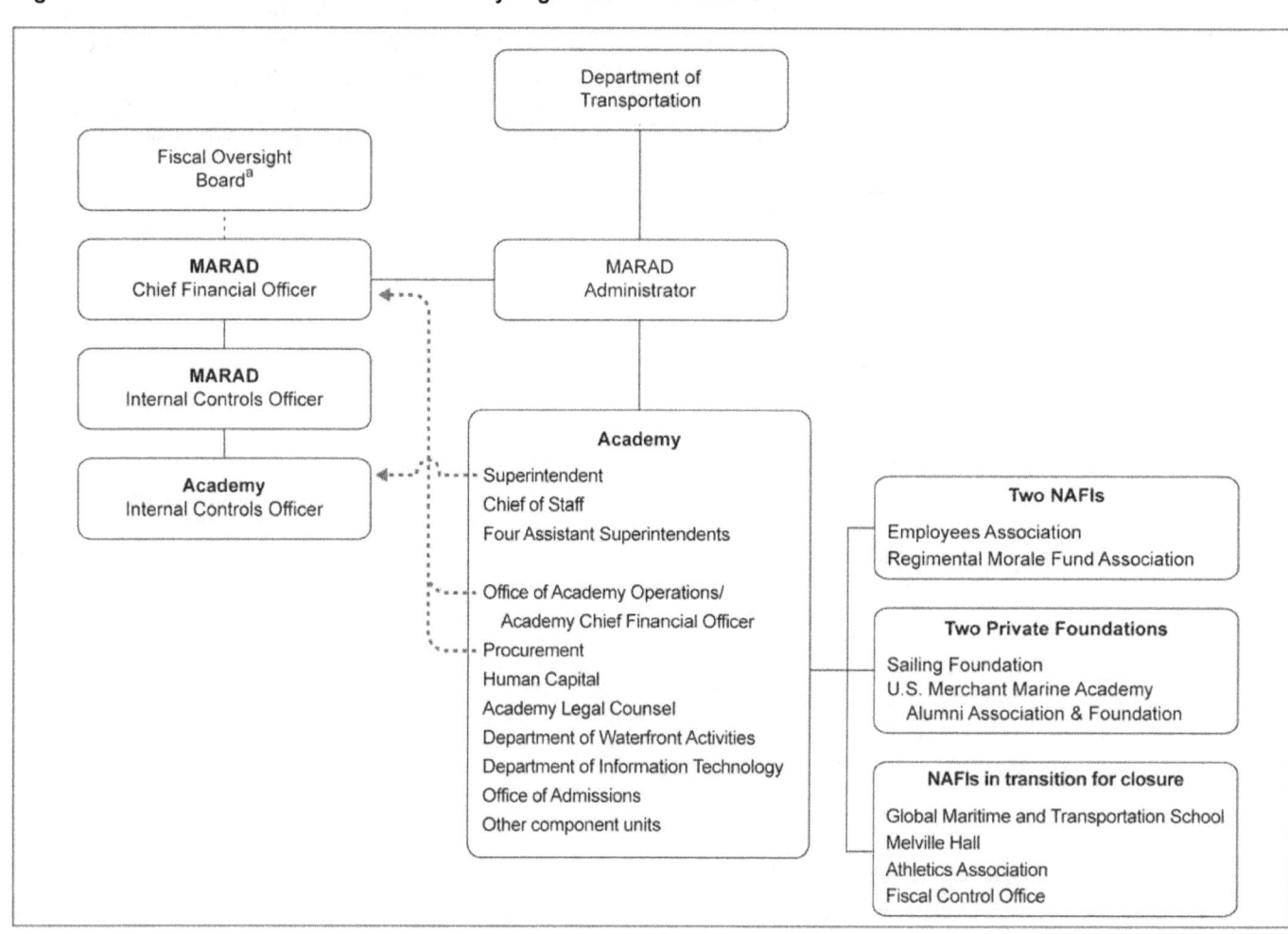

Source: GAO presentation of MARAD data as of September 2011.

[a]The Fiscal Oversight Board, comprising senior management officials from the Academy and MARAD, met on a regular basis to increase the flow of information between the Academy and MARAD. A DOT official informed us that after September 30, 2011, the Fiscal Oversight Board meetings had been replaced by weekly meetings to be chaired by the DOT Secretary and attended by departmental executives, the Maritime Administrator, and the Interim Superintendent to address Academy management issues. Additionally, the official stated that departmental executives conduct biweekly meetings with MARAD and Academy management to discuss facilities management and capital improvement issues.

GAO's 2009 Report Recommendations

Our 2009 report[6] on the Academy identified numerous internal control deficiencies as well as weaknesses in the Academy's control environment. Specifically, we found that flawed design and implementation of internal controls were the root causes of the Academy's inability to prevent or detect numerous instances of improper and questionable sources and uses of funds that we identified. Additionally, we found that the Academy lacked an accountability structure that clearly defined organizational roles and responsibilities; policies and procedures for carrying out its financial stewardship responsibilities; an oversight and monitoring process; and periodic, comprehensive financial reporting. As a result, our 2009 report included a total of 47 recommendations for corrective action.

Of the 47 recommendations, we made 1 overarching recommendation concerning actions needed for the Academy to establish effective overall internal control. Specifically, we recommended that the Secretary of Transportation direct the Administrator of MARAD, in coordination with the Superintendent of the Academy, to establish a comprehensive, risk-based internal control system to address the core causes of the control deficiencies identified in our 2009 report, including delineating the roles and responsibilities of management and employees to establish and maintain a positive and supporting attitude toward internal control and conscientious management, and the responsibility of managers to monitor control activities.

The remaining 46 recommendations related to control deficiencies associated with the following activities:

- Academy training vessel use,
- personal service acquisitions,
- NAFI camps and clinics using Academy facilities,
- midshipmen fee accountability,
- accountability for Academy reserves,
- Academy and NAFI governance structure,
- financial reporting,
- fund accountability, and
- capital asset repairs and improvements.

---

[6]GAO-09-635.

Actions Taken to Address Prior Recommendations

Our review of the Academy's and MARAD's efforts to address the issues reported in our 2009 report found that the Academy and MARAD had not yet established a comprehensive, risk-based system of internal control at the Academy. The Academy and MARAD both focused their initial efforts on the more readily correctible deficiencies in the Academy's controls over specific activities. As a result, the Academy and MARAD had made substantial progress in addressing weaknesses related to specific control activities by successfully implementing 32 of the 46 control deficiency-related recommendations identified in our 2009 report. For example, the corrective actions taken to improve controls were sufficient for us to conclude that all recommendations related to training vessel use, personal service acquisitions, accountability for Academy reserves, and NAFI camps and clinics using Academy facilities were successfully implemented.

Additional Action Needed to Establish Overall, Risk-Based Internal Control System

Our review found that actions taken by the Academy and MARAD through September 30, 2011, were not sufficient to fully address our overarching recommendation related to the establishment of a comprehensive, risk-based internal control system at the Academy, a positive and supportive attitude toward internal control, and an associated system of monitoring internal control effectiveness. *Standards for Internal Control in the Federal Government*[7] provides that internal control should (1) serve as the first line of defense in preventing and detecting errors and fraud, (2) provide for an assessment of external and internal risks to the entity, and (3) provide for internal control monitoring. Monitoring is critical to ensure that findings of audits or other reviews are promptly resolved and to assess the ongoing effectiveness of controls. However, our review found that the Academy had not yet taken actions sufficient to address the core cause of many of the control deficiencies identified in our 2009 report. Understanding the causes of internal control deficiencies is critical to designing effective, risk-based controls that can help prevent questionable transactions in the future. For example, as discussed later in this report, the Academy took action to correct errors we identified in its accounting for certain capital asset repairs and improvements, but had not yet taken action to conduct an analysis, as we recommended, to identify and address the underlying causes of these errors.

---

[7]GAO/AIMD-00-21.3.1.

Nonetheless, the Academy and MARAD have taken a number of actions that represent an important first step toward focusing the top-level attention and accountability needed to establish an effective overall system of internal control for the Academy. For example, in January 2011, MARAD established and filled an Internal Control Officer (ICO) position for the Academy. The Academy ICO, who is also the Academy's Chief Information Officer, reports to MARAD's Internal Controls Program Manager and is responsible for coordinating and leading the Academy's reviews of internal controls in accordance with Office of Management and Budget (OMB) Circular A-123 and the Federal Managers' Financial Integrity Act of 1982 (FMFIA).[8] Also, in September 2011, MARAD issued guidance in MAO 400-11 intended to help clarify the Academy's oversight role and responsibilities with respect to the Academy's affiliated NAFIs.

Despite these completed actions, until Academy and MARAD officials take additional actions to fully address our recommendation in this area, their ability to ensure that Academy and MARAD management's objectives are carried out, including proactively identifying and correcting control deficiencies in a timely fashion, will continue to be impaired. Both the Academy and MARAD focused their initial efforts on the more readily correctible deficiencies in the Academy's specific controls, as discussed later in this report. However, while these efforts are necessary and have a significant impact on internal control, it is important that the Academy and MARAD address the long-standing, deeply rooted causes of the specific control deficiencies we identified and establish processes to ensure that effective internal control is fully established, maintained, and monitored over time. In this regard, it is also important that the Academy and MARAD provide priority attention and focus not only on addressing questionable transactions we identified in our prior report, but also on the underlying causes of the specific errors we identified.

---

[8]31 U.S.C. §3512 et seq., commonly known as FMFIA, requires ongoing evaluations and reports of the adequacy of internal accounting and administrative control of each executive agency. The act requires the head of each agency to annually prepare a statement on the adequacy of the agency's systems of internal accounting and administrative control. OMB Circular A-123, *Management's Responsibility for Internal Control*, contains guidance for implementing FMFIA. OMB A-123 requires agency management to annually report on internal control in its performance and accountability report, including a report on identified material weaknesses and corrective actions.

Actions Taken to Address Many of Our Prior Recommendations Related to Specific Control Activities

As of September 30, 2011, Academy and MARAD officials had taken sufficient actions to address 32 of our 46 prior recommendations intended to address specific deficiencies in the Academy's control activities. For example, officials took steps to fully close all of our previous recommendations related to controls over training vessel use, personal service acquisitions, accountability for Academy reserves, and NAFI camps and clinics using Academy facilities. For the 14 remaining recommendations, we identified varying levels of action in process as of September 30, 2011, but none sufficient for us to consider them effectively implemented. Our conclusions on the status of Academy and MARAD actions to address our 46 previous recommendations concerning specific deficiencies in control activities are summarized in table 2, discussed in summary in the following sections, and discussed in greater detail in appendix II. *Standards for Internal Control in the Federal Government*[9] provides that agencies should take appropriate follow-up actions to address findings and recommendations of audits and other reviews. Also, GAO's *Internal Control Management and Evaluation Tool* provides that in taking such actions, agencies are to ensure that the underlying causes giving rise to the findings or recommendations are investigated, that actions are decided upon to correct the identified weaknesses, and that weaknesses are corrected promptly.[10]

Table 2: Summary of GAO Conclusion on Status of Actions Taken to Address Our 2009 Recommendations Related to the Academy's Specific Control Activities

Academy control activity	Total recommendations	Recommendations implemented	Remaining open recommendations
Training vessel use	5	5	0
Personal service acquisitions	2	2	0
NAFI camps and clinics using Academy facilities	3	3	0
Midshipmen fee accountability	9	7	2
Accountability for Academy reserves	4	4	0

[9]GAO/AIMD-00-21.3.1.

[10]GAO, *Internal Control Management and Evaluation Tool*, GAO-01-1008G (Washington, D.C.: August 2001).

Academy control activity	Total recommendations	Recommendations implemented	Remaining open recommendations
Academy and NAFI governance structure	8	4	4
Financial reporting	5	2	3
Fund accountability	7	4	3
Capital asset repairs and improvements	3	1	2
Total	**46**	**32**	**14**

Source: GAO analysis of MARAD and Academy data.

- **Training vessel use.** In 2009, we reported that the Academy lacked policies and procedures and adequate internal controls over the use of Academy training vessels by outside parties. For example, we found that the usage rates for Academy training vessels were not supported and were not based on consideration of current costs of operation. The Academy and MARAD took steps to address all five of our recommendations related to internal control deficiencies regarding outside party use of Academy training vessels. In September 2010, the Academy issued Superintendent's Instruction 2010-08, which set out procedures for outside parties to use and pay for all costs associated with the use of Academy training vessels. The Academy's Department of Waterfront Activities also issued a vessel usage rate schedule in September 2010 that provided current costs of operation for use of Academy training vessels. The guidance provides base hourly, daily, and weekly billing rates that outside parties are to be charged for using the Academy's training vessels.
- **Personal service acquisitions.** In our 2009 report,[11] we identified instances in which the Academy entered into illegal personal service agreements with its NAFIs, whereby NAFI employees performed exclusively Academy functions and reported to Academy supervisors. The Academy and MARAD took actions to address both of our recommendations related to improving internal controls over personal service acquisitions. To address our recommendations, MARAD performed an analysis to identify the nature and scope of personal service arrangements in order to determine whether amounts paid by the government were consistent with the services received by the Academy. Using the results of the analysis, MARAD took action to address all personal service arrangements by either converting

---

[11]GAO-09-635.

affected NAFI employees to the civil service or transferring them to a contract. In addition, the MARAD Administrator finalized MAO 400-11 on September 30, 2011, which provided governing principles under which NAFIs must operate, including that a NAFI must have staff to conduct its daily operations, and it is not to receive any operating subsidy from the Academy other than minor incidental support. Notably, however, MAO 400-11 requires that generally, a NAFI may not provide goods or services to the Academy.[12]

- **NAFI camps and clinics using academy facilities.** In 2009, we reported that the Academy lacked policies and procedures and effective internal controls to help ensure proper accounting for the use of fees from conducting camps and clinics using Academy athletic facilities. The Academy and MARAD took corrective actions to address all three of our recommendations related to NAFI camps and clinics' use of academy facilities. Specifically, MARAD engaged the services of an independent public accounting firm to perform an analysis to identify NAFI camps, clinics, or fund-raising activities that used Academy property from fiscal years 2006 through 2008 and determine the related sources and uses of funds. Based on this analysis, it was determined that most of the revenue resulting from the camp and clinic activity was paid to the individuals responsible for conducting the activities and the residual revenue, deemed nominal, was identified to have been used to support the general activities of the NAFI conducting the camp or clinic. Also, Superintendent's Instruction 11100.1, dated May 17, 2011, established a written policy that Academy facilities will not be used for revenue-generating athletic

---

[12]MAO 400-11 provides that the Superintendent may authorize a solicitation from a NAFI for a particular purchase on an "exigent or emergency basis," but the transaction must fully comply with the Federal Acquisition Regulation (FAR). CFO Directive 4, which also requires that transactions must fully comply with the FAR, was issued on December 30, 2009. It provides that the standard under which a NAFI can offer goods or services to the Academy is that such instances should be "exception rather than routine." Upon being notified of these differing standards, MARAD stated that CFO Directive 4 was in the process of being rescinded.

camps and clinics.[13] Our review of supporting financial documents for selected 2010 and 2011 transactions did not identify any camp or clinic activity using the Academy's facilities.

- **Midshipmen fee accountability.** In 2009, we identified instances of improper and questionable sources and uses of midshipmen fees, as well as a lack of adequate procedures and controls to maintain effective accountability over the amounts charged to midshipmen and to ensure that midshipmen fees were used only for their intended purpose. The Academy and MARAD undertook a series of reviews and completed actions that addressed seven of our nine recommendations related to midshipmen fee accountability. To address our recommendations, MARAD established a baseline for items of a personal nature and related costs to be charged to midshipmen, beginning with fiscal year 2009. Following an analysis based on this baseline, MARAD determined that prior years' midshipmen fees included the costs of items that should have been paid by the Academy. Consequently, the fees collected from midshipmen over their 4-year academic program dropped from $15,500 in fiscal year 2008 to approximately $5,500 in fiscal year 2009. As a result, MARAD proposed a refund of midshipmen fees to the midshipmen who it was determined had overpaid in academic years from academic year 2003-2004 through academic year 2008-2009. In February 2012, DOT informed us that MARAD began making refunds in November 2011 and, as of January 2012, had reimbursed 83 percent of eligible refund recipients and continued with its efforts to reach the remaining refund-eligible midshipmen.

One of the two recommendations that remain open relates to establishing written policies and procedures over (1) processing of midshipmen fee collections and payments and (2) monthly reporting for midshipmen fee activity and balances. On May 26, 2010, MARAD issued MAO 400-15, providing policy guidance governing the setting,

---

[13]Superintendent's Instruction 11100.1 states that unless superseded by the Academy Superintendent, all Academy components and personnel are prohibited from using Academy facilities or resources to conduct any revenue-generating camps or clinics. The instruction further states that any superseding direction shall incorporate the elements of our recommendation, including establishing targeted internal controls, such as the required approvals; costs to be recovered by the Academy; requirements for participation by Academy employees in the activities; and other matters of importance, such as insurance requirements, security, and required accounting records on the source and uses of funds from each event.

managing, and reporting of midshipmen fees. However, this guidance did not provide detailed procedures to ensure that staff consistently and effectively process and account for midshipmen fee activities and balances. The second of these open recommendations calls for a determination of the extent to which appropriated funds and midshipmen fees collected should be used to pay for contracted medical services. On February 5, 2010, MARAD reported the results of a joint MARAD and Academy review that identified the types of medical services provided to the midshipmen, through both appropriated and nonappropriated funding, and stated that for the fiscal year 2012 budget development process, the Administrator may wish to consider guiding the Superintendent to seek alternatives to the current approach. However, as of September 30, 2011, the Academy had not yet determined the extent to which appropriated funds and midshipmen fees collected should be used to pay for contracted medical service as called for in our recommendation.

- **Accountability for academy reserves.** Our 2009 report identified inappropriate conversion of "off-book" reserves[14] accumulated from excess midshipmen fee collections, funds received from the Global Maritime and Transportation School (GMATS) NAFI for use of the Academy's facilities, and expiring appropriated funds that were deposited to a commercial bank account to fund Academy operations the following fiscal year. For example, a "Superintendent's Reserve" account was created "off book" and used to make discretionary Academy operations payments authorized by the Academy Superintendent. The Academy and MARAD have taken corrective actions sufficient to address all four recommendations related to accountability for Academy reserves. To address our recommendations, MARAD engaged the services of a public accounting firm to perform an analysis of the sources and uses of funds held in commercial bank accounts during fiscal years 2006 through 2008 to determine consistency with applicable law, regulation, or policy. A May 19, 2010, MARAD CFO memorandum on the results of the analysis stated that the review did not identify any evidence that funds were used inappropriately or for the personal benefit of any

---

[14]After the end of an academic year, the Fiscal Control Office (FCO) typically transferred the excess of midshipmen fees collected over payments made to a commercial bank account that was not reflected in the books and records of the Academy ("off book"). FCO tracked the transaction activity in the account using off-line ("cuff") records.

individual and that no inconsistency with law, regulation, or policy was identified. Accordingly, the MARAD CFO concluded that no further action was warranted. In addition, the Academy's changed business practices discontinued conversion of appropriated and nonappropriated funds to "off-book" reserves. Further, as a result of the analysis performed in response to our recommendation, a balance of approximately $3 million in the commercial bank account maintained for excess prior-year midshipmen fee collections was transferred to the U.S. Treasury to assist with the midshipmen fee refunds.

- **Academy and NAFI governance structure.** Our 2009 report found that 11 of the 14 NAFIs that provided programs and services for Academy midshipmen and employees did not have approved governing documents, such as charters and bylaws, and that the remaining 3 NAFIs performed some duties and functions that fell outside the scope of authority set forth in their governance documents. As a result, we issued eight recommendations related to improving controls over activities between the Academy and its affiliated organizations. The Academy and MARAD completed actions sufficient to address four of our eight recommendations related to Academy and NAFI governance structure. For example, on September 30, 2011, MARAD issued MAO 400-11, which provides policies and general guidelines for the establishment and governance of NAFIs and their affiliation with the Academy, including charters, bylaws, and a NAFI governing board. In addition, an independent public accounting firm's analysis of activity between the Academy and its GMATS NAFI did not identify any activity that was inconsistent with applicable law, regulation, or policy. A May 19, 2010, MARAD CFO memorandum concluded that none of the NAFI funds were used inappropriately or for the benefit of any individual and that no further action was warranted.

Two of the four recommendations that we concluded were not yet addressed relate to performing an analysis to identify each activity involving the Academy and its NAFIs and establishing formal written policies and procedures documenting the (1) planned timing of performance of each internal control procedure for each NAFI activity, (2) responsibilities for oversight and monitoring of those internal control procedures, and (3) direct, compensating, and mitigating controls for each NAFI activity. Although MAO 400-11 provides general guidance on NAFI and Academy relationships, it does not provide the necessary detailed procedures to be followed to ensure that each NAFI has a robust, risk-based system of checks and balances with the Academy for each NAFI activity as called for in our 2009 recommendation. As of September 30, 2011, we found that neither the Academy nor MARAD had performed an analysis aimed at identifying all activities between the Academy and its ongoing affiliated organizations. Without identifying such activities and their associated risks to the Academy, the Academy faces the continued risk of improper transactions.

The other two open recommendations relate to the relationship between the Academy and its GMATS NAFI. The recommendations were intended to address the Academy improperly entering into sole-source agreements with GMATS to provide training to other federal agencies and improperly accepting and using nonappropriated GMATS funds. On September 30, 2011, the Maritime Administrator issued a memorandum rescinding the authority of GMATS to operate as a NAFI effective August 1, 2012. The memorandum also provided that GMATS may continue future operations if it is reestablished under a different operating model. However, because GMATS NAFI operations have not yet been terminated or reestablished, our two recommendations in this area remain open.

- **Financial reporting.** In 2009, we found that the Academy did not routinely prepare financial reports presenting information on all of its financial activities, including sources and uses of its appropriated and nonappropriated funds. Instead, we found that the Academy's financial reporting was sporadic, unreliable, and, consequently, of limited value for decision making. The Academy and MARAD completed actions sufficient to address two of our five recommendations aimed at improving controls over the Academy's financial reporting. MARAD issued CFO Directive 2 in December 2009 and amended it twice in 2010. Directive 2 established procedures for monitoring Academy financial performance by requiring the Office of Academy Operations to prepare, review, and provide monthly financial reports to the MARAD CFO for review. Directive 2 also provided for following up on, and documenting, unusual items and balances.

  The three recommendations that remain open relate to (1) the production of financial reports to facilitate oversight and monitoring of actual and budgeted amounts of revenues and expenses, reporting of amounts for activities and balances with affiliated organizations, and the identification of items of revenue and expenses; (2) identification and evaluation of potential misstatements of amounts in Academy financial records; and (3) compliance with required annual reporting to

Congress on all expenditures and receipts for the Academy and its affiliated organizations. CFO Directive 2 provides instructions for the Office of Academy Operation's preparation, review, and monitoring of monthly financial reports on funds allotted[15] to the Academy. However, it does not require the monthly reports to include information on all sources and uses of other funds benefiting the Academy, such as

- obligation and expenditure activity of expired funds;
- CIP and gift and bequest expenditure activity for years following obligation;
- activity for miscellaneous receipts, such as transfer of funds from closed commercial bank accounts, fees from foreign midshipmen and for outside use of training vessels, and payments from the Navy Exchange;
- sources and uses of funds maintained in commercial bank accounts; and
- sources and uses of midshipmen fees processed through two appropriation accounts and one nonappropriation account.

The MARAD CFO told us that the primary intent of Directive 2 is to report the status of funds allotted to the Academy, but acknowledged that any additional funds should be identified and reported as well. Accordingly, the MARAD CFO agreed that CFO Directive 2 reporting requirements should be updated to require all sources and uses of Academy funds to be identified and reported to provide visibility over all Academy accounts and activities necessary to facilitate comprehensive oversight and monitoring.

---

[15]An allotment is an authorization by either the agency head or another authorized employee to his/her subordinates to incur obligations within a specified amount within the requirements in OMB Circular No. A-11. The amount allotted by an agency cannot exceed the amount of appropriations that are apportioned. Apportionment is a plan, approved by OMB, to spend resources provided by one of the annual appropriations acts, a supplemental appropriations act, a continuing resolution, or a permanent law (mandatory appropriations). The apportionment identifies amounts available for obligation and expenditure. It specifies and limits the obligations that may be incurred and expenditures made (or makes other limitations, as appropriate) for specified time periods, programs, activities, projects, objects, or any combination thereof. An apportioned amount may be further subdivided by an agency into allotments, suballotments, and allocations. An allotment is part of an agency system of administrative control of funds whose purpose is to keep obligations and expenditures from exceeding apportionments and allotments.

With respect to our recommendation to identify and evaluate potential misstatements of amounts in Academy financial records, MARAD engaged an independent public accounting firm to determine the extent of any such misstatements. The review identified approximately $1.3 million in Academy expenditures funded by midshipmen fees that should have been funded by appropriated funds. However, as of September 30, 2011, MARAD had not yet determined whether it should adjust financial records and reports to reflect the use of midshipmen fees to augment Academy appropriations. MARAD officials acknowledged the need to perform additional work to determine whether adjustments to the Academy's financial records and reports are warranted.

In response to our recommendation to provide Congress a statement on the purpose and amount of all expenditures and receipts of nonappropriated funds benefiting the Academy and its affiliated organizations, MARAD issued CFO Directive 3 on December 29, 2009. Directive 3 established procedures for reporting on resources other than the Academy's appropriated funds to be included in MARAD's annual report to Congress. Specifically, the directive provides for reporting on the amount, source, intended use, and nature of such funds. However, based on our review of MARAD's fiscal year 2009 annual report to Congress—the most recent report available as of September 30, 2011—the report did not contain expenditure information for any of the Academy's affiliated organizations and did not provide a purpose for which the expenditures were made to comply with the reporting requirement as we recommended.

- **Funds accountability.** In 2009, we found that the Academy did not have assurance that it complied with applicable funds control requirements, including those in the Antideficiency Act (ADA). The Academy and MARAD have taken sufficient actions to implement four of our seven prior recommendations related to funds accountability. Specifically, officials investigated and mitigated a potential ADA violation, completed a series of reviews aimed at resolving past deficiencies related to "parking" of Academy funds to keep them from expiring,[16] and established written policy on the accrual of items of expense at year-end. With respect to the potential ADA violation, MARAD's Chief Counsel determined in 2011 that Academy officials had retained approximately $200,000 in excess funds from GMATS which they had no legal authority to retain and had thereby augmented Academy funds in excess of appropriations made by Congress during fiscal years 2006, 2007, and 2008. According to an April 11, 2011, memo signed by the Maritime Administrator, MARAD determined that sufficient prior-year funds existed to offset the GMATS-funded Academy expenditures. MARAD adjusted its accounts accordingly and since these sufficient prior-year funds existed, MARAD did not exceed its available appropriations in violation of the ADA. Also, the Academy and MARAD successfully implemented two recommendations related to "parking" of appropriated Academy funds by performing a series of reviews to identify excess Academy funds improperly held in commercial bank accounts. As a result of these reviews, the Fiscal Control Office NAFI returned over $214,000 of improperly held excess fiscal years 2006 and 2007 funds to the Academy. The Academy subsequently deobligated these funds and returned them to their respective appropriation. Further, the Academy and MARAD have discontinued use of the Academy's in-house fund control system and have transitioned to DOT's financial accounting system and have revised the Budget Program Accounting Codes. These actions should provide more transparent financial reporting and improved oversight. Additionally, in January 2010, MARAD issued CFO Directive 6 establishing policy and procedures for accounting and recording of Academy accrual of expenses at year-end. If fully and effectively implemented, Directive 6 should improve internal control over accounting and recording of Academy accrual of expenses.

The three recommendations that remain open in this area relate to

- making final notification to Congress of an ADA violation resulting from midshipmen fees that were used to cover Academy expenses without legal authority to do so,

---

[16]"Parking" of funds describes a federal entity's transfer of funds to a revolving fund or, in the Academy's case, a NAFI bank account, in an effort to keep the funds available after their period of availability expires. However, such transfers do not extend the period of availability for the transferred funds.

- implementing corrective actions as a result of a MARAD review in which it identified weaknesses related to the Academy's funds control process, and
- establishing targeted internal controls, such as management's review and approval procedures, over accruals.

According to a March 23, 2011, memorandum to the Maritime Administrator from MARAD's Chief Counsel, the Academy violated the ADA by charging midshipmen fees in excess of authorized levels, improperly augmenting agency appropriations, and making expenditures in excess of and in advance of appropriations. As of June 1, 2012, the required ADA report to Congress had not been filed. Additionally, the Academy and MARAD had yet to implement corrective actions as a result of a review of the Academy's funds control process. Specifically, on February 1, 2010, the MARAD CFO completed a review of the Academy's funds control process and made five recommendations for process improvements, including that the MARAD CFO issue a directive establishing policy and procedures requiring the periodic review and closeout of undelivered orders. The review also recommended that the MARAD CFO issue policy guidance to address an internal control weakness regarding contracting officer approval of Academy invoices. However, as of September 30, 2011, the MARAD CFO had not issued any guidance in this area. While MARAD officials told us they had practices in place for contracting officer approval of invoices, we found that as of September 30, 2011, MARAD had not documented and disseminated these practices to Academy acquisition staff in policy guidance, such as a CFO directive.

- **Capital asset repairs and improvements.** Our 2009 report identified repair and maintenance (R&M) costs that were improperly charged against the Academy's no-year[17] capital asset improvement appropriation and found that the MARAD CFO did not conduct timely reviews of the Academy's capital improvement-related expenses for fiscal years 2006 and 2007. The Academy and MARAD have taken corrective action to address one of the three recommendations we made to improve specific controls related to capital asset repairs and improvements. On May 25, 2010, the MARAD CFO issued Directive

---

[17]Capital improvement funds are provided under appropriations that remain available for an indefinite period.

7, requiring monthly review of recorded amounts of Academy repairs and maintenance expenses and capital improvement transactions to identify any anomalies, discrepancies, or questionable entries. Our work found that the Office of Academy Operations reviewed the accounting records on a monthly basis in accordance with Directive 7.

The two recommendations that remain open relate to (1) establishing policies and procedures for reporting financial information on R&M expenses and capital asset additions to help monitor these items and (2) performing an analysis to identify the causes of approximately $8 million of errors in recording R&M expenses identified in our 2009 report. While CFO Directive 7 required monthly reporting, we found that the reports were not distributed to users, such as Academy department managers, to facilitate monitoring of these items as called for in our recommendation. With respect to our recommendation to identify the causes of the errors in recording R&M expenses, we found that the Academy and MARAD had taken action to reclassify the transaction errors we identified but had not yet conducted the recommended root cause analysis needed to identify and address any systemic issues causing the errors and to prevent such errors in the future. Consequently, the Academy and MARAD are at risk of reoccurrences of errors in R&M expense accounting.

Further Enhancements to Capital Improvement Program Oversight Are Needed

Although the Academy and MARAD have taken steps to improve oversight of the Academy's CIP, the Academy does not have a current comprehensive plan for capital improvements to provide the basis for oversight of CIP planning and implementation. In response to a May 2009 directive from the Secretary of Transportation, MARAD convened an independent "Blue Ribbon" advisory panel consisting of senior government executives to analyze the Academy's CIP and its investment priorities. The panel concluded that the Academy's facilities were seriously deteriorated and its support buildings were inadequately maintained. The panel's March 2010 report, *USMMA: Red Sky in the Morning*,[18] provided 11 recommendations, which included linking a comprehensive Academy strategic plan to its Facilities Master Plan with capital investments prioritized for a 10- to 15-year period to address the Academy's extensive needs. According to DOT officials, MARAD

---

[18]U.S. Merchant Marine Academy Capital Improvements Advisory Panel, *USMMA: Red Sky in the Morning*, March 2010.

prepared its *USMMA Capital Improvements Implementation Plan*[19] in November 2010 to serve as a road map for implementing the panel's recommendations and to identify the Academy's immediate capital improvement needs through 2016.

The Academy also established and filled a new position for an Assistant Superintendent for Capital Improvements and Facilities Maintenance in 2010, designating the new position's responsibilities to include oversight of the Academy's Departments of Capital Improvements and Facilities Maintenance and the Office of Safety and Environmental Protection. This position is to provide oversight for the Academy's CIP and leadership for strategic planning and accountability related to capital improvement activities. Further, according to Academy officials, the Academy realigned its facilities management organizational structure in December 2010 to reflect that of other academic organizations and service academies and to improve oversight.

Despite these recent improvements, the Academy has not yet developed reliable project cost estimates and current phased capital investment plans aligned with the organization's strategic objectives, as recommended by the Blue Ribbon panel in 2010. Guidance issued by OMB as well as our prior work on leading practices in this area identifies the need for effective capital planning to provide CIP accountability and oversight. Our *Executive Guide: Leading Practices in Capital Decision-Making*[20] summarizes the results of our research on leading capital planning practices used by state and local government and private-sector organizations. It includes practical steps for implementing capital planning effectively and presents examples that illustrate and complement many of the concepts and specific steps contained in OMB's *Capital Programming Guide.*[21] Our *GAO Cost Estimating and Assessment Guide,*[22] which

---

[19]Maritime Administration, *USMMA Capital Improvements Implementation Plan*, November 2010.

[20]GAO, *Executive Guide: Leading Practices in Capital Decision-Making*, GAO/AIMD-99-32 (Washington, D.C.: December 1998).

[21]OMB, *Capital Programming Guide: Supplement to Circular A-11, Part 7, Preparation, Submission, and Execution of the Budget* (Washington, D.C.: Executive Office of the President, August 2011).

[22]GAO, *GAO Cost Estimating and Assessment Guide: Best Practices for Developing and Managing Capital Program Costs*, GAO-09-3SP (Washington, D.C.: March 2009).

provides best practices for developing, managing, and evaluating capital program cost estimates, complements the *Executive Guide*. Fundamental success factors identified in our *Executive Guide* include developing long-term capital investment plans that integrate with long-range organizational strategic objectives, present reliable project cost estimates to inform decision making, and use a phased priority approach to guide and schedule capital spending.

The Academy's Facilities Master Plan, which identified anticipated capital projects for a 10-year period in three priority phases, has not been comprehensively updated since 2002. Up-to-date CIP information that identifies and prioritizes long-range renovation and new construction projects and provides reliable project cost estimates and completion and funding timelines would facilitate oversight by helping to assess whether individual improvements were carried out in a timely and cost-effective manner and in priority order. We identified instances where improvements were not carried out in priority order and also identified lengthy delays in completing some planned capital investments. For example, the 2002 Facilities Master Plan showed that the midshipmen's primary commissary, Delano Hall (which serves over 2,000 meals a day to the Academy's residential midshipman population), was to have been refurbished during fiscal year 2002. As of September 30, 2011, the Delano Hall refurbishment project had not yet broken ground. According to information that DOT provided in February 2012, several tasks related to the Delano Hall refurbishment project have been completed, such as remodeling rest rooms in compliance with the Americans with Disabilities Act. DOT told us at that time that it expected construction on the commissary to begin in the summer of 2012 and to be completed by December 2013.

Preparing the 2010 *Capital Improvements Implementation Plan* was a positive step, although the implementation plan acknowledged the need for a more comprehensive, phased investment plan. For example, the implementation plan did not present a long-range phased investment plan and detailed cost estimates. Rather, projects presented were based on average replacement cost per square foot for federal government buildings, described in the plan as a "rough order of magnitude estimate." Accordingly, the cost estimates presented in the implementation plan did not consider specific cost factors for capital improvements at the Academy, such as geographic location, local cost of construction and labor, and the technology, simulation, and infrastructure requirements of an institution of higher education. As stated previously and recommended by the 2010 Blue Ribbon panel, reliable cost estimates and phased investment priorities for Academy capital projects that are aligned with the organization's long-range strategic objectives would help facilitate CIP oversight. According to DOT officials, the Academy had recently begun preparing its first strategic plan to define the organization's goals and objectives and to help the Academy better prioritize investments. Specifically, they told us in February 2012 that the strategic planning process for the Academy is to be led by the Academy's Acting Superintendent and is expected to be a multiphased effort beginning with identification of key internal stakeholders to assist with the development of critical issues that should be addressed in the strategic plan.

Conclusions

Clearly articulated top management vision and support will be critical for fully implementing the open recommendation related to establishing a comprehensive risk-based system of internal control and related monitoring. The Academy and MARAD have taken a number of positive steps, but until Academy and MARAD officials take additional actions to fully address our recommendation in this area, their ability to ensure that management's objectives are carried out, including proactively identifying and correcting control deficiencies in a timely fashion, will continue to be impaired. We reiterate the need to continue efforts to complete full implementation of this recommendation. The Academy and MARAD have made significant progress in addressing our prior recommendations related to specific control activities, and their actions effectively addressed 32 of the 46 recommendations related to deficiencies in specific controls. We reiterate the need to address the remaining 14 recommendations related to midshipmen fee accountability, Academy and NAFI governance structure, financial reporting controls, fund accountability, and controls over capital asset repairs and improvements.

The Academy and MARAD have taken steps to improve CIP oversight and planning of capital improvement projects at the Academy. However, the Academy does not have comprehensive, updated information on capital improvement projects, including reliable cost data, long-range capital investment plans, and phased priorities. Further, the Academy has not yet aligned its capital improvement priorities with the organization's strategic objectives, a critical factor in providing effective oversight.

Recommendation for Executive Action

To improve oversight of the Academy's capital improvement program, we recommend that the Secretary of Transportation direct MARAD to work with Academy officials to develop and maintain a current and comprehensive plan in accordance with leading practices and guidance. At a minimum, such plan should include

- an inventory of long-range capital improvements that align with the Academy's strategic objectives,
- reliable estimates of cost specific to each capital improvement, and
- a phased investment approach for prioritizing capital improvement needs.

Agency Comments and Our Evaluation

On June 19, 2012, DOT provided written comments on a draft of this report, signed by the Deputy Assistant Secretary for Administration. The comments are reprinted in appendix III. In its comments, DOT described steps that the department, MARAD, and Academy are taking to help prioritize and manage Academy capital improvement projects. DOT indicated that these actions are aligned with and fulfill the recommendation in our draft report. Specifically, DOT stated that since our draft report was issued, the department, MARAD, and the Academy established a comprehensive CIP that includes a Senior Advisory Council and working group; a management process that provides a clear and consistent understanding of project status; and controls for project selection, management, and completion, including tracking reports, process documentation, and Senior Advisory Council meetings to monitor progress.

We are encouraged by the increased oversight these measures would provide for the Academy's capital investments. However, it is too soon to determine the extent to which the new CIP addresses the three specific elements that our recommendation provided as minimum attributes for a comprehensive capital improvement plan: an inventory of long-range capital improvements that align with the Academy's strategic objectives, reliable cost estimates specific to each capital improvement, and a phased investment approach for prioritizing capital improvement needs. We believe these attributes are critical to facilitating oversight of the Academy's capital improvements to ensure that they address the needs of the midshipmen in accordance with the strategic vision of the Academy, are undertaken in priority order, and are completed timely and cost effectively.

DOT also stated that it remains dedicated to the challenging task of building and operating a comprehensive system of internal controls at the Academy, including completing action on all recommendations in our prior report, and will keep us apprised of progress to close out our recommendations. DOT further stated that it has established a goal of completing action on all 46 of our specific control-related recommendations by December 31, 2012.

We are sending copies of this report to the Secretary of Transportation; Maritime Administrator; and Superintendent, U.S. Merchant Marine Academy. In addition, the report will be available at no charge on the GAO website at http://www.gao.gov.

If you or your staff have any questions concerning this report, please contact me at (202) 512-9500 or DavisBH@gao.gov. Contact points for our Offices of Congressional Relations and Public Affairs may be found on the last page of this report. GAO staff who made key contributions to this report are listed in appendix IV.

Beryl H. Davis
Director
Financial Management and Assurance

Appendix I: Scope and Methodology

To address our objective to assess the extent to which actions have been taken to address our prior recommendations as contained in our report, *United States Merchant Marine Academy: Internal Control Weaknesses Resulted in Improper Sources and Uses of Funds; Some Corrective Actions Are Under Way* (GAO-09-635), we interviewed agency officials and reviewed and analyzed

- MARAD summaries of action steps taken in response to our recommendations;
- activities and policies, procedures, and memorandums issued by the U.S. Merchant Marine Academy (Academy) and Maritime Administration (MARAD); and
- laws and regulations governing Academy operations.

In addition, as part of our assessment of recommendations related to accountability for Academy reserves, financial reporting controls, and fund accountability, we obtained a database of Academy obligations and expenditures at the transaction level for fiscal years 2010 and 2011 to make a nonstatistical selection of transactions to obtain an understanding of the Academy's accounting process. We compared these data to amounts reported for the Academy in the Department of Transportation's (DOT) annual performance and accountability reports. We performed system walk-throughs to gain an understanding of procedures in place. As part of this assessment, we reviewed and analyzed

- receipts and disbursements records;
- bank statements; and
- procurement documentation for selected transactions, including contracts, purchase orders, receiving documentation, invoices, and disbursement documents and other pertinent supporting documents.

We also reviewed and discussed with appropriate officials the objectives and scope of a report prepared by an independent public accountant engaged by MARAD on its analysis of certain prior-year sources and uses of funds that related to our recommendations.

Further, for some specific recommendations, we reviewed rate schedules, billings and underlying calculations, payroll records, and congressional notifications, as appropriate. We also reviewed analyses prepared by the Academy, MARAD, and certain nonappropriated fund instrumentalities (NAFI) regarding specific transaction types, such as a midshipmen fee refund schedule and a summary of payments made by the Global Maritime and Transportation School (GMATS) NAFI to the Academy.

To assess actions taken to address our recommendations regarding controls over financial reporting and capital asset repairs and improvements, we also reviewed monthly reports summarizing transaction activity and balances.

To address our second objective regarding our assessment of oversight of the Academy's Capital Improvement Program (CIP), we interviewed Academy and MARAD officials and reviewed Academy and MARAD procedures, monthly reports to MARAD, and monthly analyses prepared to help ensure that transactions are accounted for properly. We also reviewed the Academy's 2002 Facilities Master Plan, a report on the Academy's CIP prepared by a Blue Ribbon panel,[1] a follow-up implementation plan that responded to the Blue Ribbon panel report,[2] and GAO and Office of Management and Budget (OMB) guides related to capital improvements project planning. We also observed the Academy's physical plant.

We evaluated corrective actions taken through September 30, 2011, that the Academy, MARAD, and DOT made us aware of by February 15, 2012. In addition, we reviewed DOT's Office of Inspector General audit and investigation reports for the period from January 2010 through March 2012 to determine if any work related to the Academy had been performed. No audit reports that could have an impact on this engagement were noted.

We conducted this performance audit from February 2011 to June 2012 in accordance with generally accepted government auditing standards. Those standards require that we plan and perform the audit to obtain sufficient, appropriate evidence to provide a reasonable basis for our findings and conclusions based on our audit objectives. We believe that the evidence obtained provides a reasonable basis for our findings and conclusions based on our audit objectives.

---

[1]U.S. Merchant Marine Academy Capital Improvements Advisory Panel, *Red Sky in the Morning*, March 2010.

[2]Maritime Administration, *USMMA Capital Improvements Implementation Plan*, November 2010.

Appendix II: Status of Prior Recommendations and Description of Corrective Actions Taken

This appendix presents a list of the 47 recommendations that we previously issued in our August 2009 report[1] along with our analysis of the implementation status of each recommendation (see table 3). We evaluated corrective actions taken through September 30, 2011.

Table 3: Implementation Status of GAO Recommendations

Recommendation	Status per GAO
Overall internal control and monitoring – To improve the design and operation of the internal control system at the Academy, we recommend that the following actions be taken.	
1. Establish a comprehensive risk-based internal control system that addresses the core causes and the challenges to proper administration that we identify in this report, including the risks and challenges that flow from the close organizational and transactional relationships between the Academy and its affiliated organizations and implement internal controls that address the elements of our *Standards for Internal Control in the Federal Government*, including the role and responsibilities of management and employees to establish and maintain a positive and supportive attitude toward internal control and conscientious management, and the responsibility for managers and other officials to monitor control activities.	**Open.** As of September 30, 2011, the Academy had not yet established a comprehensive risk-based internal control system to include monitoring to ensure ongoing effectiveness and efficiency of operations, reliability of financial reporting, and compliance with laws and regulations. In contrast to the substantial actions taken to address many of the deficiencies concerning specific Academy control activities, few corrective actions have yet been taken to address the fundamental weaknesses we previously identified concerning the Academy establishing a comprehensive risk-based internal control system and monitoring. In particular, the Academy had not addressed the underlying causes of many of the deficiencies we identified in the Academy's specific control activities. MARAD officials told us that these overriding deficiencies were not yet addressed because their strategy has been to focus on the deficiencies that could be more readily resolved—those relating to deficiencies in controls over specific Academy activities.
Training vessel use – To improve internal controls over activities from usage of training vessels and other Academy-owned boats by others, the Academy should take the following actions:	
2. Perform an analysis to identify all activity involving the use of the *Kings Pointer* and Academy-owned boats by others, including all sources and uses of funds for fiscal years 2006 and 2007. • Identify and recover the cost of any unreimbursed nongovernmental uses, to the extent authorized by law. • For each payment, including payments to affiliated organizations, that is determined to be for other than a proper governmental purpose and that is not consistent with law, regulation, and policy, consider pursuing recovery from the organization or individual that benefited from the payment.	**Closed.** MARAD engaged an independent public accountant to identify activities related to the use of Academy-owned training vessels by outside parties and identify the sources and uses of funds, including the bank accounts used in these transactions for fiscal years 2006, 2007, and 2008. On April 30, 2010, the independent public accountant completed its analysis and concluded that it did not identify any payments that could be characterized as being for other than the continuing operations of the Academy or for the benefit of the midshipmen. On September 21, 2010, the Acting MARAD Chief Financial Officer (CFO) also concluded that funds from the usage of training vessels were used only for the benefit of the Academy or its midshipmen. Based on the independent

---

[1]GAO, *United States Merchant Marine Academy: Internal Control Weaknesses Resulted in Improper Sources and Uses of Funds; Some Corrective Actions Are Under Way*, GAO-09-635 (Washington, D.C.: Aug. 10, 2009).

Recommendation	Status per GAO
	public accountant's work, MARAD management determined that no further actions were warranted. We are closing this recommendation because the independent public accountant's analysis performed did not identify any misuse of government funds during fiscal years 2006 through 2007. We also noted that the Academy's changed business practices include new written policies and procedures that govern the use of Academy training vessels.
3. Establish written policies and procedures to govern the use of the Academy-owned training vessel, the *Kings Pointer*, and other boats, including addressing issues for ships' crews, insurance, security, billing procedures, and other responsibilities.	**Closed.** On September 29, 2010, the Academy issued Superintendent's Instruction 2010-08, which established policies and procedures governing the use of Academy-owned training vessels by outside parties. The instruction contained the process by which Academy-owned training vessels would be made available to outside parties and stated that all costs associated with their use shall be borne by the outside user—including the cost of personnel, fuel, provisions, dockages, and maintenance and repair.
4. Perform or contract out a comprehensive usage rate study to establish usage rates. Such a study should include (1) consideration of the full cost to the Academy of the training vessels and other boats, including salaries and benefits of Academy personnel, major repairs, routine maintenance, nonroutine maintenance and long-term repairs, fuel, and dockage, and (2) identification of indirect expenses and imputed costs as appropriate (e.g., depreciation).	**Closed.** On September 29, 2010, the Academy's Department of Waterfront Activities completed a usage rate study and issued a vessel usage rate schedule, entitled *Usage Rates for T/V* Kings Pointer *and Other USMMA Vessels*, establishing a base hourly, daily, and weekly billing rate for use of Academy-owned training vessels by outside parties. The base rate includes direct and indirect costs related to the ship's crew, administrative personnel, major repairs, routine maintenance, and operational expenses. Fuel charges are to be billed on a direct reimbursable basis.
5. Establish policy for the timing and extent of the analysis required for periodic updates to the usage rate study.	**Closed.** On September 29, 2010, the Academy issued Superintendent's Instruction 2010-08, which required the Director of Waterfront Activities to maintain a comprehensive schedule of usage rates for all Academy vessels made available for use by outside parties. Additionally, the instruction states that the schedule may be adjusted for cost-of-living, inflation, or payroll increases on an annual basis, and shall be reviewed for other factors at least every 3 years. Prior to completion of our review, and as a result of our transaction testing results, the Academy updated the usage rate policy and reissued it on July 20, 2011.
6. Determine—in coordination with the department or MARAD legal counsel, as appropriate—if the Academy had the legal authority to retain and use any collections from the use of the Academy-owned training vessel the *Kings Pointer* and other boats; otherwise, deposit them in the general fund of the U.S. Treasury.	**Closed.** In fiscal years 2006 and 2007, MARAD's appropriations acts permitted MARAD to collect moneys for utilities, services, and necessary repairs in connection with any lease, contract, or occupancy and credit these funds back to the appropriation charged. However, any portions of rental receipts for items other than utilities, services, or repairs were to be deposited into the Treasury as miscellaneous receipts. Although there was authority to take up certain collections from the use of Academy-owned training vessels and other boats and credit these funds back to the appropriation charged, it was not possible to definitely determine whether MARAD's treatment of its collections was in accordance with its authority because available records do not

Recommendation	Status per GAO
	detail the sources of all funds and financial records do not detail their complete application. MARAD stated that it would develop recommendations for further improvement of the record-keeping process, and that it was proceeding with the development of a written lease to be employed in all instances of vessel use by outside parties.

Personal service acquisitions – To improve accountability and internal controls over the acquisition of personal services from NAFIs, and to resolve potential issues surrounding past personal services activities and payments, the Academy should take the following actions:

Recommendation	Status per GAO
7. Perform an analysis to identify the nature and full scope of personal services activities and the associated sources and uses of funds to include a review of all questionable payments, including those that we identify in this report for personal services totaling more than $8 million for fiscal years 2006 and 2007. For each such personal services arrangement, (1) determine if the amounts paid were consistent with the services received by the Academy; (2) quantify the amounts, if any, paid by the Academy for personal services that were not received by the Academy; and (3) document the decisions made with respect to any payments by the Academy for personal services that were not received, including decisions to seek recovery from other organizations for such amounts.	**Closed.** On February 25, 2010, the MARAD CFO issued a memo to the Fiscal Oversight Board (FOB) summarizing a follow-up review that had identified 15 NAFI positions that were paid all or in part with the Academy's appropriations but had not been identified in an earlier review, which resulted in the conversion of NAFI staff to civil service or contract positions. The memo described the disposition of those positions and identified 3 positions funded with appropriations that performed functions exclusively for the NAFIs. The follow-up review also determined that the amounts rendered were consistent with the services received by the Academy; however, the MARAD CFO concluded that there was no possibility of recovering the amounts paid for these positions from the organizations that benefited. We are closing this recommendation based on (1) the results of the analysis MARAD performed and (2) the Academy's changed business practices with the implementation of Maritime Administrative Order (MAO) 400-11 and the discontinued use of illegal personal service arrangements.
8. Develop written policy guidance on acquiring services from NAFIs that complies with the requirements of law, regulation, and policy on the proper use of funds by the Academy.	**Closed.** On September 30, 2011, MARAD issued MAO 400-11, which provided governing principles under which NAFIs must operate. It included principles stating that a NAFI, generally, may not provide goods or services to the Academy; must have staff to conduct its daily operations; and will receive no operating subsidy from the Academy, in kind or otherwise, other than minor incidental support. In addition, Section 6.03 of the MAO states the charters and bylaws of authorized NAFIs will provide for oversight by a three-person Governing Board made up of members approved by the Maritime Administrator and Academy Superintendent. The NAFI Governing Board is to be accountable for ensuring that the Academy's NAFIs are operated consistently with the governing principles set forth by MAO 400-11.

NAFI camps and clinics using academy facilities – To improve internal controls over camps and clinics operated by the Athletics Association NAFI or others on Academy property, the Academy should take the following actions:

Recommendation	Status per GAO
9. Perform an analysis to identify practices at the Academy involving camps and clinics operated by the Athletics Association or others using Academy property and other assets. Document the nature and scope of such activities, including all sources and uses of funds for fiscal years 2006 and 2007, and take corrective action on any improper transactions.	**Closed.** MARAD engaged an independent public accountant to identify camps, clinics, or similar fund-raising activities operated by the Athletics Association using Academy property; document the scope and nature of these activities, including the sources and uses of funds; and document payments to coaches constituting their compensation for fiscal years 2006, 2007, and 2008. Based

Recommendation	Status per GAO
	on this analysis, MARAD management issued a memo on May 13, 2010, stating that the majority of the camps and clinics revenue had been provided to the individuals conducting the camps and clinics and that the residual revenue had been minor and was used to support the general activities of the Athletics Association. We are closing this recommendation because the analysis performed did not identify any misuse of government funds during fiscal years 2006 through 2008. Also, we noted that the Academy's business practices have changed with the establishment of Superintendent Instruction 11100.1, stating that it is the official policy of the Academy that its facilities will not be used for revenue-generating athletic camps or clinics. Our review, which included physical observation and review of financial documents for selected 2010 and 2011 transactions, did not identify any camp and clinic activities or revenue related to such activities.
10. Establish written policies and procedures for camps and clinics operated by the Athletics Association NAFI or others on Academy property.	**Closed.** Superintendent's Instruction 11100.1, dated May 17, 2011, established written policy that Academy facilities will not be used for revenue-generating athletics camps and clinics. Our work, which included physical observation and review of financial documents for selected 2010 and 2011 transactions, did not identify any camp and clinic activities or revenue related to such activities.
11. Establish targeted internal controls that include approvals required; costs to be recovered by the Academy; requirements (such as advance approval) for participation by Academy employees in the activities; and other matters of importance, such as insurance requirements, security, and required accountings to be provided to the Academy on the sources and uses of funds from each event.	**Closed.** The Academy has terminated all camp and clinic-related activities. Superintendent's Instruction 11100.1, dated May 17, 2011, established written policy that Academy facilities will not be used for revenue-generating athletics camps and clinics. Our work, which included physical observation and review of financial documents for selected 2010 and 2011 transactions, did not identify any camp and clinic activities or revenue related to such activities.
Midshipmen fee accountability – To improve accountability and internal controls over midshipmen fee activities and to resolve potential issues surrounding the past collections and uses of midshipmen fees, the Academy should take the following actions:	
12. Perform an analysis to identify all midshipmen fee collections for fiscal years 2006, 2007, and 2008, to include identifying those items for which the fee collected is attributable to (1) an activity between the midshipmen as customers and a NAFI as service provider (e.g., collections for haircuts) and (2) an activity between the midshipmen as customer and the Academy as service provider (e.g., collections for personal computers). Determine if the (1) fee collected for each item was for a personal item of the midshipmen and consistent with law, regulation, and policy for such collections; (2) amount of the fee collected for each item was properly supported, based on, among other things, an analysis of the cost to the Academy for the good or service; and (3) amount collected exceeded the cost of the good or service. Further, determine if any liability may exist for collections that (1) are not consistent with law, regulation, and policy as personal items of the midshipmen; (2) were not properly supported, in	**Closed.** MARAD engaged an independent public accountant to perform an analysis to identify midshipmen fee collections and uses of collected funds for academic years 2003—the first year for which Academy accounting records were considered reliable—through 2009. The analysis was to identify any questionable payments, or categories of payments, that may not be consistent with law, regulation, or policy, and calculate an amount that MARAD management could consider as a potential refund to the midshipmen. On April 30, 2010, the independent public accountant completed its analysis and provided the results to MARAD and was able to account for almost all of the fee revenue collected. The independent public accountant provided MARAD with a spreadsheet model to estimate elements of cost data that were incomplete for some academic years. Supplementing this spreadsheet analysis with a trend analysis prepared by the

Recommendation	Status per GAO
whole or part; and (3) exceeded the cost to the Academy for the good or service.	MARAD CFO, MARAD determined the amount collected that exceeded the cost of goods and services provided to midshipmen. Based on the calculated excess collections, the Academy implemented a program to reimburse overcharges to midshipmen from 2003 through 2008.
13. Perform an analysis to identify all payment activity and other uses of the funds collected for midshipmen fees for fiscal years 2006, 2007, and 2008, to include reviewing payment activity to identify the payees, amounts, and other characteristics of the uses of the funds collected and conducting a detailed review of payment activity and other uses (e.g., transfers to prior years' reserves) for items considered as high risk. • Review all questionable payments and other uses of funds, such as transfers to commercial checking accounts for the excess of collections over funds used, as well as the questionable payments that we identify in this report. • For each payment and other use of funds that is determined to be for other than a proper governmental purpose and that is not consistent with law, regulation, and policy, consider pursuing recovery from the organization or individual that benefited from the payment.	**Closed.** MARAD engaged an independent public accountant to perform an analysis to identify midshipmen fee collections and uses of collected funds for academic years 2003 through 2009. The analysis was to identify any questionable payments or categories of payments that may not be consistent with law, regulation, or policy. On April 30, 2010, the independent public accountant provided MARAD with the results of its analysis, which did not identify any payments that could not be fairly categorized as supporting the continuing operations of the Academy or for the benefit of the midshipmen. A September 16, 2010, memorandum signed by the Acting MARAD CFO stated that based on the totality of the work performed, including previous work performed by the MARAD CFO's Office and the independent public accountant, nothing had come to MARAD's attention related to improper payments that would warrant a recovery of funds. We are closing this recommendation because the independent public accountant's analysis did not identify any misuse of government funds during 2006 through 2008. Additionally, we noted that the Academy changed business practices, discontinuing the use of commercial bank accounts to manage midshipmen fee collections and documenting policy to establish the baseline items due from midshipmen, the amount of fees to be collected, and the approved uses of such fees.
14. Establish policies and procedures and perform the necessary analysis to support annual reports to the Congress to address changes in "any item or service" in midshipmen fees from that existing in 1994 as required by law.	**Closed.** On May 26, 2010, MARAD issued MAO 400-15, requiring that the MARAD CFO ensure that the Academy complies with the annual midshipmen fee reporting requirement established in 46 U.S.C. § 51314. This section requires the Secretary of Transportation to notify Congress of any change made by the Academy in the amount of a charge or fee charged to a midshipman at the Academy. Further, we obtained and verified DOT's November 23, 2009, and September 10, 2010, notifications to Congress regarding the changes in the midshipmen fee schedule for academic years 2009–2010 and 2010–2011.
15. Establish written policy and criteria for determining the baseline items that are properly due from midshipmen for personal items, the amount of fees to be collected (based on underlying studies), and the approved uses of the fees collected.	**Closed.** On May 26, 2010, MARAD issued policy in MAO 400-15 establishing seven baseline categories of personal goods and services that the Academy may provide to midshipmen and for which the Academy may collect and use midshipmen fees. The policy also provides guidance on how the fee amounts are to be determined. Additionally, we verified that the Academy had established and revised the amount of fees to be charged for each of the baseline categories for academic years 2009–2010 and 2010–2011 in accordance with the policy.

Recommendation	Status per GAO
16. Establish written policy for the underlying analysis that is required and the approvals that must be obtained before changes are made in the baseline of midshipmen fee items, or before a change is made in the amount of such fees, or in the approved uses of the fees collected.	**Closed.** On May 26, 2010, MARAD issued MAO 400-15, establishing written policy for, among other things, the analysis and approvals required to change the baseline items for which collection and use of midshipmen fees are authorized. Specifically, in advance of each academic year, the Superintendent is required to develop a midshipmen fee schedule based upon input from Academy program offices for approval by the Maritime Administrator. No fees are to be charged without the Administrator's approval. Any request to the Administrator to impose, collect, and use fees for goods and services in addition to the seven categories of baseline items identified in the MAO is to be made through the MARAD CFO.
17. Utilize the information obtained from the analysis of midshipmen fees collected in prior years and other work to determine the amount of midshipmen fees that should be charged to midshipmen for personal items in subsequent years.	**Closed.** In May 2009, MARAD, working in conjunction with the Academy, issued a revised midshipmen fee schedule for academic year 2009, which reduced midshipmen fees by approximately 64 percent compared to those of the prior fiscal year. Information obtained from the independent public accountant's midshipmen fee analysis and MARAD's cost trend analysis for academic years 2003 through 2009 provided the basis for the schedule. By academic year, the schedule presented items of a personal nature that became the personal property of midshipmen but were procured by the Academy. Further, MAO 400-15 provides that because of inflation and price fluctuations on actual purchases and services, midshipmen fees are reviewed and adjusted each academic year. Specifically, in advance of each academic year, the Academy Superintendent shall develop a midshipmen fee schedule based on input from Academy program offices for approval by the Maritime Administrator. While conducting our review at the Academy, we verified that the billings to midshipmen were based on the published rates. Also, we obtained the revised midshipmen fee schedule for academic year 2010–2011 to validate that the schedule was updated to reflect actual, current prices of the goods and services provided to the midshipmen when compared to the revised 2009 midshipmen fee schedule.
18. Establish policies and procedures that require those charged by the Academy with the responsibility for midshipmen fee collections and payments to (1) maintain detailed accounting records for all midshipmen fee activities that reflect accurate and fully supported information on collections, payments, and other activities that is consistent with document retention practices; (2) implement written review and approval protocols for all midshipmen fee collections and uses of funds consistent with policies and procedures established by the Academy and MARAD; and (3) provide monthly detailed reports of all midshipmen fee activities in the aggregate and by item to Academy and MARAD officials.	**Open.** The Academy and MARAD have taken several actions to address this recommendation. MARAD issued a policy in MAO 400-15, issued in May 2010, to address the handling, usage, and reporting of midshipmen fees. Among other things, the MAO addressed policy regarding written protocols for the collection and use of midshipmen fees, accounting for the fees, reviews of fee collection and uses, and requirements for monthly detailed reports of all midshipmen fee activities to Academy and MARAD officials. Also, in accordance with the fiscal year 2010 Consolidated Appropriations Act, the Academy must now credit midshipmen fee collections to MARAD's Operations and Training account with the U.S. Treasury to assist in tracking and accounting for midshipmen fee activities in DOT's accounting system. Further, MARAD issued CFO Directive 2 in December 2009, establishing required procedures for the Office of Academy Operations to produce

Recommendation	Status per GAO
	monthly Academy financial reports for review by Academy and MARAD officials, including information regarding the status of midshipmen fees. However, our walk-through of the midshipmen fee collections process demonstrated the complex series of steps Academy staff use to maintain detailed accounts of individual midshipmen fee activity and balances, which includes manual entry of transactions in a system separate from the Academy general ledger system. At the time of this walk-through, the Academy was operating without documented detailed accounting procedures for maintaining detailed accounts of individual midshipmen fee activity and balances.
19. Establish written policy for internal reviews of monthly reports of midshipmen fee activity and balances, identified anomalies, and questioned items as well as the results from the associated follow-up.	**Closed.** MARAD issued CFO Directive 2 establishing written policy for internal reviews of monthly reports of midshipmen fee activity. Directive 2 also established written policy requiring the Office of Academy Operations to identify any anomalies requiring additional information, follow-up, or action. Further, the Office of Academy Operations is to document the written records, with associated disposition, of any identified anomalies.
20. Perform an analysis to determine whether and, if applicable, the extent to which appropriated funds and midshipmen fees collected should be used to pay for contracted medical services.	**Open.** As of September 30, 2011, neither MARAD nor the Academy had performed an analysis to determine the extent to which midshipmen fees and appropriated funds should be utilized to pay for contracted medical services. However, memorandums from the FOB Chair to the Maritime Administrator document FOB conversation and consideration of this matter and a conclusion that for the fiscal year 2012 budget development process, the Administrator may wish to consider alternatives to the current approach.
Accountability for academy reserves – To address funds held in commercial bank accounts of the Fiscal Control Office (FCO) from prior years' reserves and Superintendent's Reserves and to resolve issues surrounding the past collections and uses of funds for excess midshipmen fee collections, the Academy should take the following actions:	
21. Perform an analysis to identify all activities in the prior years' and other reserves, including all sources and uses of funds for fiscal years 2006, 2007, and 2008. • Review all the questionable payments and other activity, including payments that we identify in this report that according to FCO records total $605,347. • For each payment that is determined to be for other than a proper governmental purpose and that is not consistent with law, regulation, and policy, consider pursuing recovery from the organization or individual that benefited from the payment.	**Closed.** MARAD engaged an independent public accountant to perform an analysis to identify the sources and uses of funds held in the commercial bank accounts of the FCO NAFI for fiscal years 2006, 2007, and 2008, including the $605,347 we previously identified. The funds—or Superintendent's Reserves—included in the review were GMATS Reserves, the Year-End Appropriated Funds Reserve, and the Excess Midshipmen Fees Reserve. In addition, the independent public accountant reviewed collections and expenditures of the FCO commercial bank accounts that could not be attributed to any of the Superintendent's Reserves. On April 30, 2010, the independent public accountant provided MARAD with the results of its analysis, which identified examples of typical uses of the funds, including payments for telephone and cable services, accounting software, express mail services, and office equipment—all purposes consistent with the Academy's mission or support of the midshipmen through its NAFIs. We are closing this recommendation because the analysis performed by the independent public accountant did not identify any misuse of

Recommendation	Status per GAO
	government funds during fiscal years 2006 through 2008. Also, we noted that the Academy's changed business practices have discontinued conversion of appropriated and nonappropriated funds to "off-book" reserves.
22. Investigate the unexplained $100,000 transaction(s) in September 2007 per the off-line or "cuff" accounting records maintained by FCO and take actions as appropriate.	**Closed.** MARAD engaged the services of an independent public accountant to investigate the unexplained transactions totaling $100,000 in the Academy's FCO NAFI off-line record of monthly activity. On April 30, 2010, the independent public accountant report did not identify any express evidence of fraud. We are closing this recommendation because the Academy and MARAD conducted an investigation of the unexplained transactions. We also noted that the Academy changed its business practices—discontinuing the conversion of available funds to "off-book" reserves and eliminating "cuff" accounting systems.
23. Finalize actions to protect and recover Academy funds held in commercial bank accounts by the FCO from current and prior years' midshipmen fees that totaled approximately $2 million at September 30, 2008.	**Closed.** On June 7, 2009, the Academy CFO took steps to secure prior-year excess balances in midshipmen fees held in commercial bank accounts by the FCO and protect excess balances from the academic year ending June 2009—which totaled approximately $3 million by that time. The excess midshipmen fees were to remain frozen until the approval of a methodology and procedures to use these funds to refund the overcharged midshipmen.
24. Require that (1) bank reconciliations be prepared for all activity in the commercial bank accounts of the FCO used for these reserves during fiscal years 2006, 2007, and 2008; (2) documentation be prepared for all questionable items as well as the related follow-up; and (3) going forward, such bank reconciliations be timely prepared and independently reviewed by Academy staff with no direct involvement in the reconciliations or the activity in the bank accounts.	**Closed.** MARAD engaged an independent public accountant to perform the reconciliation as called for in this recommendation. The analysis was to include sufficient detail on the uses of funds to identify any specific questionable payments or categories of payments and facilitate documentation and follow-up on such items. On May 19, 2010, the MARAD CFO issued a memo concluding that—based on the totality of the work that the independent public accountant performed—there was no indication that these funds were used inappropriately or for the personal benefit of any individual. MARAD issued CFO Directive 2, which established procedures for the Academy's CFO to reconcile transaction activity in all commercial bank accounts. The Academy CFO is to also prepare an exhibit for inclusion in the Academy's monthly financial report that confirms reconciliations were performed on the bank accounts.
Academy and NAFI governance structure – To improve internal controls over activities with its affiliated organizations, we recommend that the Academy take the following actions:	
25. Perform a comprehensive review and document the results of an analysis of the risks posed by the Academy's organizational structure and its relationships with each of its affiliated organizations, including address the inherent organizational conflicts of interest that we identify in this report regarding Academy managers having responsibility for activities with affiliated organizations that are in conflict with the managers' Academy responsibilities, and determine whether the current organizational structure should be maintained or whether an	**Closed.** We believe the intent of this recommendation has been met because the Academy and MARAD assessed the Academy/NAFI relationship and demonstrated a commitment to improving the Academy's organizational structure. This was sufficiently demonstrated through evidence in the form of decision memos; charters; bylaws; MAO 400-11; and the closure or planned closure of 10 NAFIs, including GMATS, Melville Hall, and the Athletics

Recommendation	Status per GAO
alternative organizational structure would be more efficient and effective, while at the same time reducing risk and facilitating improvement in internal control and accountability.	Association. These changes should allow for more efficient and effective operations, as well as assist in reducing risk and facilitating improvements in internal control and accountability.
26. Require that all affiliated organizations have approved governing documents and that the functions they will perform in the future are consistent with their scope of authority.	**Closed.** On September 30, 2011, MARAD issued MAO 400-11, which provides governing principles and the governance structure of the two remaining NAFIs—the Employees Association and the Regimental Morale Fund Association. The MAO requires the establishment of charters, bylaws, and a NAFI governing board, as well as an annual business plan detailing the NAFIs' proposed programs of activities, resource needs, anticipated operating expenses, and financial plans for the current and forecasted 2 years.
27. Perform an analysis to identify all activities between the Academy and the NAFI, GMATS, during fiscal years 2006 and 2007 and determine for each activity the nature of the activity; the amounts collected by the Academy or others for the benefit of the Academy; the nature and amounts paid, by the Academy or by others for the benefit of the Academy, from the funds collected; the business purpose; the reason for Academy involvement; and if the activity complies with law, regulation, and policy.	**Closed.** MARAD engaged an independent public accountant to identify GMATS funds that were made available from its two reserves to support the Academy's operations. The Superintendent's Reserve consisted of funds received from GMATS and deposited into a NAFI bank account for use at the Superintendent's discretion. The GMATS Reserve, which was used at the discretion of various Academy officials, consisted of funds made available to the Academy from the GMATS bank account and was intended to serve as indirect compensation for GMATS use of Academy facilities. The independent public accountant's analysis of the Superintendent's Reserve concluded that no payments could be specifically characterized as being for other than the continuing operations of the school or for the benefit of the midshipmen. The analysis of the GMATS Reserve concluded that payments were related to the business of the Academy and for the benefit of the school in all cases. MARAD legal analysis determined that sufficient prior-year unobligated appropriated funds were available to offset the GMATS-funded expenditures during each fiscal year in question, mitigating the potential for an Antideficiency Act (ADA) violation and any reporting requirements. We are closing this recommendation because (1) the analysis performed did not identify any misuse of government funds during fiscal years 2006 through 2008 and (2) the Academy's business practices in this area have improved.
28. Consider pursuing recovery from the organization or individual that benefited from the payment for each payment that is determined to be for other than a proper governmental purpose and that is not consistent with law, regulation, and policy.	**Closed.** The independent public accountant's analysis of the Superintendent's and GMATS Reserves determined that no payments could be specifically identified for anything other than the continuing operations of the school or the benefit of the midshipmen. We are closing this recommendation because the analysis performed did not identify any misuse of government funds during fiscal years 2006 through 2008. Also, we noted that the Academy improved its business practices by discontinuing acceptance, deposit, and conversion of GMATS funds.
29. Perform an analysis to identify each activity involving the Academy and its affiliated organizations and for each activity	**Open.**

Recommendation	Status per GAO
determine the business purpose; the reason for Academy involvement; the business risk that each activity presents; and if the activity complies with law, regulation, and policy. Design a robust system of checks and balances for each activity with each affiliated organization that is consistent with the business risk that each activity presents, considering, among other things, the nature and volume of the activities with each affiliated organization.	As of September 30, 2011, the Academy had not performed an analysis identifying activities between the Academy and its affiliated organizations that would allow—in addition to the identification of the attributes listed in the recommendation—the design of a robust system of checks and balances for each activity identified. To its credit, MARAD has established charters and bylaws for the two remaining NAFIs; issued a policy statement that to the extent practicable, the NAFIs should produce an annual business plan addressing their proposed programs of activities; and issued CFO Directive 4, which reiterated the requirement to conduct procurement transactions in accordance with Federal Acquisition Regulation (FAR) requirements. However, this order lacks the necessary detailed procedures, such as documenting the planned timing of performance, documenting monitoring responsibilities, and defining appropriate controls for each ongoing NAFI activity.
30. Establish formal written policies and procedures for each activity involving the Academy and an affiliated organization and specify for each activity the required documentation requirements, necessary approvals and reviews, and requirements for transparency (e.g., require regular financial reports for each activity for review and approval by Academy management and MARAD officials charged with oversight). Establish internal controls for each activity with each affiliated organization, including (1) the planned timing of performance of the control activity (e.g., periodic reconciliations of billings with collections); (2) the responsibilities for oversight and monitoring and the documentation requirements for those performing oversight and monitoring functions; and (3) the necessary direct, compensating, and mitigating controls for each activity.	**Open.** As of September 30, 2011, the Academy had not performed an analysis identifying activities between the Academy and its affiliated organizations that would facilitate the establishment of formal, written policies and procedures for each activity between the Academy and its affiliated organizations. Although MARAD made some progress by issuing MAO 400-11—which provided guidelines for the establishment, governance, and maintenance of NAFIs—the MAO does not provide the necessary detailed procedures as called for in our recommendation.
31. Establish formal written policies and procedures that among other things, specify the allowable activities and transactions between the Academy and GMATS, and detail the necessary approvals and reviews required for each activity.	**Open.** On September 30, 2011, the Maritime Administrator issued a memo, which stated that the NAFI is not an appropriate operating model for GMATS and rescinded its authority. It authorized continued transitional operations to allow GMATS to complete and deliver training classes through July 31, 2012. By December 30, 2011, the Academy Superintendent, in coordination with the MARAD CFO, was to prepare an implementation plan for the orderly shutdown of the GMATS NAFI, with an option for the plan to include the GMATS plans for any future activities under a new operating model. However, because the GMATS NAFI operations have not yet been terminated or reestablished, this recommendation remains open.
32. Establish targeted internal controls for each direct and indirect activity between the Academy and GMATS.	**Open.** On September 30, 2011, the Maritime Administrator issued a memo, which stated that the NAFI is not an appropriate operating model for GMATS and rescinded its authority. It authorized continued transitional operations to allow GMATS to complete and deliver training classes through July 31, 2012. By December 30, 2011, the Academy Superintendent, in coordination with the MARAD CFO, was to prepare an implementation plan for the

Recommendation	Status per GAO
	orderly shutdown of the GMATS NAFI, with an option for the plan to include the GMATS plans for any future activities under a new operating model.
	However, because the GMATS NAFI operations have not yet been terminated or reestablished, this recommendation remains open.
Financial reporting controls – To improve internal controls over financial information, the Academy should take the following actions:	
33. Implement comprehensive policies and procedures for the review of financial reports, to include requiring reviews by the preparers of the financial reports as to their completeness and accuracy; evidence of departmental management reviews; and written records of identified anomalies and questioned items, as well as requirements for maintaining evidence of the results from associated follow-up on all identified anomalies and questioned items.	**Closed.** MARAD issued CFO Directive 2 in October 2010 to provide instructions for the preparation, review, and monitoring of Academy monthly financial reports. In accordance with CFO Directive 2, the Office of Academy Operations provides a memo to the MARAD CFO documenting the Academy's review of financial reports each month. The memo identifies which Academy senior staff participate in each review and summarizes related discussions covering areas concerning senior managers and the Academy's unresolved business. The Academy's Assistant CFO maintains evidence of follow-up to these discussions.
34. Implement financial reporting policies and procedures that among other things, will provide visibility and accountability to Academy activities and balances to facilitate oversight and monitoring, including (1) periodic reporting of actual and budget amounts for revenues and expenses for the current and cumulative period; (2) periodic reporting of amounts for activity and balances with affiliated organizations in detail; and (3) identification of items of revenue and expense for each funding source, including annual and no-year appropriated funds and other collections.	**Open.** Although MARAD issued CFO Directive 2 in October 2010 to provide instructions for the preparation, review, and monitoring of monthly financial reports, our transaction testing demonstrated that not all financial activity is accounted for in the monthly reports. For example, as of September 30, 2011, we found that the monthly reports did not include information on (1) obligation and expenditure activity of expired funds; (2) CIP and gift and bequest expenditure activity for years following obligation; (3) activity for miscellaneous receipts, such as transfer of funds from closed commercial bank accounts, fees from others' use of Academy training vessels, and payments from the Navy Exchange; (4) sources and uses of funds maintained in commercial bank accounts; and (5) sources and uses of midshipmen fees processed through two appropriation accounts and one nonappropriation account.
35. Identify and evaluate the potential misstatements of amounts in the financial records for the Academy in fiscal years 2006, 2007, and 2008 to determine if restatement or reassurance of budget and financial reports and statements prepared from those records is appropriate, including (1) $5,076,198 of errors in accounting for repairs and maintenance expenses and capital additions, and $3,431,725 of expenses that were improperly funded with no-year capital improvement appropriations; (2) $6,410,242 and $6,038,061 of recorded revenue and expenses, respectively, from GMATS training programs; (3) amounts for midshipmen fee collections and payment activity, including effects on reported revenues, expenses, assets, and liabilities; and (4) amounts for sources and uses of funds handled "off book" that	**Open.** On September 17, 2010, the Acting MARAD CFO issued a memorandum stating that adjustments to the fiscal years 2008 and 2009 accounting records were made to correct the errors in Academy accounting for repairs and maintenance expenses and capital asset additions, as well as the funds handled "off book," including transactions in the three Superintendent's Reserves, as available records allowed. With respect to recording revenue and expenses from GMATS training programs, MARAD recognized the Academy's error but noted that because correcting the offsetting revenue and expense amounts in MARAD's Statements of Net Costs would not have any impact on MARAD's future financial statements, it declined to make adjustments for fiscal years 2006 and 2007. Further, MARAD noted that as a consolidated part of DOT's financial statements, the restatement would not be needed because these adjustments are below

Recommendation	Status per GAO
we identify in this report, including transactions in three Superintendent's Reserves and with GMATS and FCO.	DOT's restatement threshold (i.e., $500 million). However, with respect to the third aspect of this recommendation, midshipmen fee collections, MARAD engaged the services of an independent public accountant to determine the source and use of midshipmen fees for academic years 2003 through 2009, which identified approximately $1.3 million in Academy expenditures funded by midshipmen fees that should have been funded with appropriated funds. As of September 30, 2011, MARAD had not yet determined whether adjusting entries were required to reflect the use of midshipmen fees to augment Academy appropriations.
36. Implement policies and procedures to obtain the information necessary to timely comply with the requirement identified in the 2009 report for annual reports to the Congress that provides all expenditure and receipt information for the Academy and its affiliated organizations.	**Open.** On December 29, 2009, MARAD issued CFO Directive 3, establishing procedures for the production of a report on resources other than the Academy's appropriated funds—such as gifts and bequests received by the Academy and paid to others, midshipmen fee receipts and expenditures, and GMATS receipts and expenditures—to be included in MARAD's annual report to Congress. However, the directive does not include sufficiently detailed procedures on the data to be provided for inclusion in the report and does not address all aspects of the reporting requirement. Although the MARAD CFO told us that the annual report to Congress fulfills the requirement, we found that the fiscal year 2009 report lacked expenditure information for any of the Academy's affiliated organizations and the purposes for which the expenditures were made. As of February 2012, MARAD's fiscal year 2010 annual report to Congress was not available for review.
37. To improve the design and operation of the internal control system at the Academy, implement a program to monitor the Academy's performance, including reviews of periodic financial reports prepared by Academy officials and reviews of the Academy's documentation and analysis from its review of its periodic financial reports and associated items, such as the results of its follow-up on unusual items and balances.	**Closed.** The Academy issued CFO Directive 2 in December 2009, establishing procedures for the production of monthly Academy financial reports that were to be provided to cognizant Academy offices and departments and the MARAD Office of the Budget to assist in their performance oversight. The reporting requirements included documenting identified anomalies and questioned items and their resolution. Directive 2 was revised twice in 2010, expanding the information required to be reported each month. Further, a review of the previous 12 months' reporting for the fiscal year ended September 30, 2011, demonstrated that the monthly reports were reviewed by the Academy CFO and associated follow-up was performed on any identified unusual items and balances.
Fund accountability – To determine whether the Academy complied with the ADA,[a] the Academy should take the following actions:	
38. Determine whether legal authority exists to retain payments to the Academy from GMATS, both in Academy appropriations accounts and in commercial bank accounts of affiliated organizations, and if not, adjust the Academy's appropriations accounts to charge available Academy appropriations and expense accounts for the amounts of official Academy expenses that were paid by funds received from GMATS or paid directly by GMATS on behalf of the Academy. To the extent that insufficient appropriations remain available for these expenses, report ADA violations as required by law.	**Closed.** The MARAD Chief Counsel determined that Academy officials retained excess funds for which they had no legal authority and augmented funds in excess of appropriations made by Congress. Specifically, during fiscal years 2006, 2007, and 2008 the Academy accepted payments from and on behalf of GMATS totaling approximately $200,000. According to the facts collected and provided by MARAD's Office of the CFO, the Academy violated the miscellaneous receipts statute by failing to deposit the GMATS funds into the U.S. Treasury and, instead, depositing

Recommendation	Status per GAO
	funds into commercial bank accounts to use at Academy discretion. Additionally, it was determined the Academy "utilized funds provided by [GMATS] so as to augment the funding made available ... by Congress." The funds were used in place of the Academy's Operations & Training appropriation. In an April 11, 2011, memo signed by the Maritime Administrator, MARAD determined that sufficient prior-year funds existed to offset the GMATS-funded expenditures. MARAD adjusted its accounts accordingly, and since sufficient prior-year funds existed, MARAD did not exceed its available appropriation in violation of the ADA.
39. Perform an analysis to identify all activities involving accrual accounts used to "park" appropriated funds with the FCO, including all sources and uses of funds for fiscal years 2006 and 2007.	**Closed.** MARAD's Assistant CFO for Academy operations analyzed the Academy's year-end transactions for fiscal years 2005 through 2007 to identify activities involving accrual accounts utilized to "park" appropriated funds within the NAFI FCO. Two summary memos—dated June 5 and 6, 2008—explained that the review had resulted in over $214,000 of fiscal year 2006 and 2007 funds being returned from the FCO NAFI to the Academy and that the Academy had deobligated the funds.
40. Consider pursuing recovery from the organization or individual that benefited from the payment for each payment that is determined to be for other than a proper governmental purpose.	**Closed.** Based on the Academy, MARAD, and the independent public accountant's analysis of the year-end appropriated funds held in a FCO reserve bank account, MARAD did not identify any payments not related to the continuing operations of the school or for the benefit of the midshipmen. As a result, On May 19, 2010, the MARAD CFO concluded that—based on the totality of the work performed by the independent public accountant and the Academy—nothing was brought to light to suggest these funds were used inappropriately or for the personal benefit of any individual. We are closing this recommendation because the analysis performed did not identify any misuse of government funds during fiscal years 2006 through 2007. Additionally, we noted that the Academy's changed business practices address the practice of "parking" appropriated funds within accrual accounts of the FCO.
41. Determine the amounts of midshipmen fees that were used to cover official Academy expenses without legal authority to do so and adjust the Academy's accounts, as necessary, to charge available appropriations for such expenses. To the extent that insufficient appropriations remain available, report ADA violations as required by law.	**Open.** In a March 23, 2011, memorandum from MARAD's Chief Counsel to the Maritime Administrator it was determined that officials at the Academy violated the ADA by charging midshipmen fees in excess of authorized levels, improperly augmenting agency appropriations, and made expenditures in excess of and in advance of appropriations. The total amount of the augmentation was estimated to be $8.13 million over 6 academic years, beginning in academic year 2003–2004. As of March 23, 2011, the MARAD CFO determined the Treasury fee account held $3.12 million attributable to excess midshipmen fee collections. Application of the $3.12 million in excess fees held by the Treasury to the $8.13 million debt left a $5.01 million deficiency. DOT received a deficiency appropriation from Congress of up to $6 million to be used to reimburse the full estimated amount of overcharges to midshipmen for academic years 2003–2004 through 2008–2009. The required ADA report pending final DOT

Recommendation	Status per GAO
	approval prior to submission to Congress had not been filed as of June 1, 2012.
42. To provide reasonable assurance that the Academy will comply with the Antideficiency Act and other applicable laws and regulations, we recommend a review of the funds control process be performed at the Academy and corrective actions be taken on any identified deficiencies.	**Open.** On February 1, 2010, the MARAD CFO submitted the results of a review of the Academy's funds control processes to the Acting Maritime Administrator. The review made numerous recommendations for process improvements. For example, the review recommended that the MARAD CFO issue a CFO directive establishing a policy and procedure requiring the periodic review and closeout of undelivered orders. As of September 30, 2011, the MARAD CFO had not yet issued the related policy. The review also recommended issuing policy guidance regarding contracting officer approval of Academy invoices. DOT officials told us the procedure regarding contracting officer approval of Academy invoices was prepared as part of the review of internal controls under OMB Circular A-123. However, MARAD only sent the procedure to officials within MARAD, and no formal or informal document establishing the procedure was developed and disseminated to Academy procurement personnel. Academy procurement officials we spoke with were unaware of any policy guidance related to contractor officer approval of invoices.
43. Establish written policy guidance on the accrual of items of expense at year-end.	**Closed.** On January 29, 2010, MARAD issued CFO Directive 6 providing policy guidance on the accrual of items of expense at year-end. Specifically, the directive stated that the accrual of Academy expenses should be conducted in accordance with MARAD and DOT financial policy and generally accepted accounting principles. The directive also provided the general principle that revenues should be recognized when earned and expenses should be recognized when a liability is incurred, without regard to receipts or payments of cash.
44. Establish targeted internal controls that among other things, provide the criteria for accruals, specify the documentation requirements for accruals, and provide management's review and approval procedures.	**Open.** On January 29, 2010, MARAD issued CFO Directive 6, providing overall control policy for the accrual of expenses at the Academy. However, while CFO Directive 6 is a positive step, this recommendation remains open because Directive 6 does not provide criteria or specify the documentation requirements for the accrual of Academy expenses at year-end, or identify the specific required review and approval procedures for accruals.
Controls over capital asset repairs and improvements – To improve internal controls over processing of vendor invoices and accounting for repairs and maintenance expenses and additions to capital assets, the Academy should take the following actions:	
45. Establish written policies and procedures for repairs and maintenance expenses and capital asset additions that require (1) periodic reviews of recorded amounts for repairs and maintenance expenses and capital asset additions to identify and timely address issues requiring management attention and (2) correction of errors before financial reports are prepared from the books and records.	**Closed.** On May 25, 2010, MARAD issued CFO Directive 7, requiring monthly reporting and review of Academy repairs and maintenance expenses and capital improvement transactions to identify any instances of anomalies, discrepancies, or questionable entries. During our audit, we found that the Academy CFO's Office prepared and carried out the required review

Recommendation	Status per GAO
	monthly.
46. Perform an analysis to identify the causes of the errors in the recording of repairs and maintenance expenses that should have been capitalized, totaling $5,076,198, and $3,431,725 of expenses that were improperly funded with the no-year capital improvement appropriation, during fiscal years 2006 and 2007.	**Open.** Although the Academy and MARAD reclassified certain incorrect transactions we identified in our August 2009 report, they have not yet identified the root cause(s) of these errors necessary to help guard against recurrence of such errors.
47. Establish policies and procedures for periodic reporting of financial information for repairs and maintenance expenses and capital additions to assist users in monitoring these items as well as the funding sources—annual appropriations or no-year appropriations for long-term improvement projects.	**Open.** The Academy and MARAD implemented CFO Directive 7 to address this recommendation. Directive 7 establishes procedures for distinguishing between accounting for and recording costs of Academy capital assets and ordinary maintenance and repair. It also requires monthly reports on Academy repairs and maintenance expenses and capital improvement transactions to be generated and reviewed for instances of anomalies, discrepancies, or questionable entries. While the directive is a positive step, it does not fully satisfy our recommendation. We found that the Directive 7 monthly reports were not distributed to the department-level users to allow for monitoring of repairs and maintenance expenses and capital asset additions as called for in our recommendation. Further, while the policy in Directive 7 requires that a detail report be run to validate that expenditures were recorded correctly, the Academy officials responsible for running this report did not have access to the prescribed reporting format.

Source: GAO analysis of DOT data.

[a]31 U.S.C. §§ 1341-42, 1349-51, 1511-19.

Appendix III: Comments from the Department of Transportation

**U.S. Department
of Transportation**

Office of the Secretary
of Transportation

JUN 19 2012

400 Seventh St., S.W.
Washington, D.C. 20590

Ms. Beryl H. Davis
Director, Financial Management and Assurance
U.S. Government Accountability Office
441 G Street, NW
Washington, DC 20458

Dear Ms. Davis:

The United States Merchant Marine Academy (USMMA) has provided an important service to the nation since World War II, training a dependable cadre of highly capable merchant mariners to serve the country in times of war and maintaining a viable U.S. maritime industry in times of peace. While its success at accomplishing this primary mission continues, so does the U.S. Department of Transportation's work to ensure that the USMMA achieves organizational excellence. This is being accomplished through actions completed and under way, in updating its management, policies, processes and procedures to provide effective capabilities for managing a contemporary Federal government entity.

The Secretary of Transportation and the Maritime Administrator, together with top officials throughout the Department, are dedicated to providing the USMMA with the leadership and management structure it requires. This includes building the internal controls structure it needs to function effectively and ensure that funds are fully accounted for and well spent. While much has been achieved, including recent accomplishments reached after the GAO draft report was issued, we recognize that difficult challenges remain.

The challenges enumerated in GAO's 2009 report on USMMA were formidable and extensive. In response, we applied unprecedented top management attention to tracking USMMA's and MARAD's progress in implementing the report's recommendations. Top management continues to be directly involved in, and aware of, the actions taken and the progress achieved. For example, most of the Non-Appropriated Fund Instrumentalities (NAFI) have been closed. Reimbursements of fee overpayments have been provided to 97 percent of the eligible midshipmen and USMMA graduates.

MARAD and USMMA established new policies and procedures in each of the areas addressed in the GAO report. In those cases where GAO subsequently determined that additional detail would be useful to fully achieving recommended actions, MARAD is working to complete the necessary enhancements. Further, a new management team is being put in place at USMMA, including a new Superintendent, who will be selected in the near future, to provide top-notch management skills. Additional specialized management skills in a number of critical areas including finance, technology, capital asset management, and security are also being put in place to provide expertise and leadership in fulfilling the GAO recommendations and to maintain an effective internal controls environment.

Since GAO issued its draft report, the Department, MARAD, and USMMA established a comprehensive Capital Improvement Program (CIP) to help prioritize and manage USMMA capital improvement projects. This approach includes a top management Senior Advisory Council and a working group chaired by the Deputy Assistant Secretary for Budget and Programs. The CIP established a management process that provides a clear and consistent understanding of project status and overlays effective management controls for project selection, management and completion. These controls include tracking reports, process documentation, and regular meetings of the Advisory Council to monitor progress. These actions are aligned with, and will fulfill, the recommendation included in the GAO draft report.

The Department remains dedicated to the challenging task of building and operating a comprehensive system of internal controls within USMMA, including completing action on all of the GAO recommendations. With two-thirds of the recommendations complete, and more scheduled for completion this summer, the Department has established a goal of completing action on the 46 individual recommendations by December 31, 2012. We will keep GAO apprised of our progress and provide documentation of completed actions to close out the recommendations. Once the people, policies, and processes are all in place, we will ensure that a comprehensive system for internal controls has been established that would fulfill the 47th and final recommendation from GAO's 2009 report.

We appreciate this opportunity to comment on the GAO draft report. The GAO recommendations have provided an invaluable resource for guiding our efforts. Please contact Martin Gertel, Director of Audit Relations, with any questions or if we may be of further assistance.

Brodi Fontenot
Deputy Assistant Secretary
 for Administration

Appendix IV: GAO Contact and Staff Acknowledgments

GAO Contact	Beryl Davis, (202) 512-9500 or DavisBH@gao.gov
Staff Acknowledgments	In addition to the contact named above, Jack Warner, Assistant Director; Crystal Alfred; Francine DelVecchio; Geoff Frank; Pat Frey; Matthew Gardner; Jehan Abdel-Gawad; Jamie Haynes; Kate Lenane; and Scott McNulty made key contributions to this report.

www.ingramcontent.com/pod-product-compliance
Lightning Source LLC
Chambersburg PA
CBHW080915290526
45795CB00007BA/2534